Woman of Influence

Woman of INfluence
Discover the Power and Purpose of Who You Are

Katie Walker
Philipa A. Booyens

2018

Printed in the United States of America

First Printing, 2018

ISBN 978-1-387-68831-9

www.INsightScene.com
www.afteredenmanagement.com

"You are beyond beautiful, you matter,
and you are greatly loved."

- INsight Scene

Table of Contents

Preface

Let's Take a Journey Together

Believing that you are a woman of influence, a woman that can change the course of history, for the better, takes purposive journey. This devotional will help you understand your influence, remind you whose you are in Christ, and activate you to live within your callings. It will also give you steps to encourage your relationship with the Lord while reminding you of His desire for a close, intimate relationship with you. As you go on this journey based on God's word about you, I believe you will see yourself differently, love larger, have new perspectives, and transform those around you.

I want to encourage you to meditate on these devotionals and be patient while your heart is awakened to hearing God's voice over you. You will find that He satisfies your heart, and you satisfy His. When you spend time with the Lord, you will find He is sweet, kind, and loving us through the journey of becoming more like Him.

I love that you have decided to take this journey with me, and I know when you have completed this devotional you will feel refreshed by His word, and passionate to know more of Him. He will continue to encourage you in your everyday life. Journal and pray through these words spoken over you and let your heart be teachable with faith until you realize how chosen you are, and you are here for a very important purpose for this time and this season.

-Katie Walker

How to use this devotional: This 30-day devotional was created to drive home your *value* and *influence*. Start by reading the first five chapters all the way through before beginning the daily devotionals.

~

Prayer: *May the God of all creation pour out His grace and allow revelation of who He is to penetrate the heart of every reader. May you be blessed and encouraged to live in the influence and purpose that God has given you. May you be protected from evil and may you and your family be prosperous in all you put your hands too. You are His darling, and it's time you know. In Jesus name I pray, Amen.*

Acknowledgments

With any new first time project there are many people I would like to thank personally.

Jaco and Philipa A. Booyens: Your constant encouragement, support, and love push me to reach higher, and dream beyond my ability. Without your expertise this project would not have been possible. I am blessed to call you family. Thank you. I love and appreciate you with all my heart.

The After Eden Team: You are the family that continues to blow on the burning fuse in my heart to passionately seek Christ with all my might. You've encouraged and supported me every step of the way. Much love to you all.

INsight Scene: To every women and host of INSight Scene I am eternally grateful for your love and support of this project, and your serving heart to contribute to the devotional. Your words matter, and they have blessed me more than you could ever know.

Jan Burns: My mom, who we call "Honey" in my home. I want to thank you with all my heart for being the greatest cheerleader to my every dream, a warrior intercessor, and my best friend. You know me the best, and love me anyway. The best is yet to come. I love you.

My Children: Riley, Jack, Presley, and Shea: May you continue to grow to love the Lord your God with all your heart and lean on Him with your all. May my ceiling be your floor. I love you forever.

To My Husband, Todd: When God gave me you he gave me the best. Your unconditional love and support has given me courage to step into so many new adventures. Your loyalty and support give me so much joy, and I am committed to being the best woman of influence I can be as long as I have breath. I love you!

Introduction

I've learned to like the car rides back and forth to drop kids off, or to run errands because that's where I have to eliminate all that distracts me, watch the road, and listen. I raise a small army of children from teens to tweens to young school age, so if I happen to be in the car alone, I turn the radio off and talk to God. It seems to be the place that the Lord gets my attention, and I hear His voice very clearly like I did the other day.

In the quiet, God prompted this question in my spirit, "Katie, why did Satan give the apple to a woman?"

I was taken aback and responded, "I don't know, Lord." I then waited as I knew that what would be coming next would be a revelation.

"Because Eve was an influencer. Satan knew he could get to anyone through Eve. Women are influencers. You, as women, have been given the power to affect others. How are you influencing those around you?"

Immediately, I started pondering how I had acted that day. Was I kind? Was I uplifting? Was I focused on only myself and my needs? Did I influence those around me for good or bad?

Then a thought passed through my head, quieting all the others, "Wait a minute. Do you really think you have that much power?" That question had a familiar ring to it. It reminded me of how Satan deceived Eve in the garden:

> *"But the serpent said to the woman, You shall*
> *surely not die, For God knows that in the day*
> *you eat of it your eyes will be opened, and you*
> *will be like God, knowing the difference between*

good and evil and blessing and calamity. And when the woman saw that the tree was good (suitable, pleasant) for food and that it was delightful to look at, and a tree to be desired in order to make one wise, she took of its fruit and ate; and she gave some also to her husband, and he ate." Genesis 3:4-6 [AMPC]

Notice how the serpent went to Eve. She was the first woman and the first influencer. When "...she gave some also to her husband, and he ate it," no questions were mentioned. No disputes ensued, like Eve had made with the serpent. Adam just ate it because Eve gave it to him. From the very beginning, the power we've been given to influence our world and those around us has always been clear. I think that's why the serpent - Satan - is still very focused in his attacks against women, just as he was after this revelation, trying to convince me not to believe what I was hearing from the Lord.

Knowing this, I was determined to seek Jesus with this revelation and when I did, I knew I had to share it with you.

Because, just like Esther, you were made for such a time as this (Esther 4:14b). The power and purpose of your influence has never been more important. The world we are living in is filled with hate, sin and sadness. We are living in the legacy of those with influence before us and what we do now will shape our present and the future generations. God tells us in Psalm 78 that He gave Moses His laws to be passed down from this generation to the next, even to those not born yet. By following His ways, we -- as the chosen children of God -- will break the bondage of stubborn and rebellious generations.

For if we don't recognize the power of influence we have, what we pass down will be just like the past generations whose spirits have strayed from

God, and who refused to love Him with all their hearts. We will essentially abandon the world to darkness, sin and the problems this has created.

Women are influencers. We can change this world. We need to do so and are called to do so.

This world needs you. That's why you are here. We must truly believe the promises of God over our lives, trust Him, and move forward in faith. It's time to discover and embrace all that you are called to be and move in the influence you have so that we can make the world a better place.

May this book encourage you, remind you of whose you are, teach the truth of your identity and purpose, and provide stepping stones upon the Rock to bring wisdom into your everyday life. We believe you will be filled with the overflow and abundant joy that only heaven can bring, and that God will kindle the passionate fire deep inside of you to give you new perspectives on how valuable you are. You are a priceless treasure. Your words matter. You are not alone or forgotten. You are chosen and here in this world because God said the world needed your influence to continue His purpose for us all: to know Him in all His wonder!

Without further ado, it's time to discover and embrace the power and purpose of who you are.

Chapter 1

Women Are INfluencers
You have great power and responsibility

Women have a long history of being attacked and oppressed. In the most subtle and the most blatant of ways we've been told what to wear, what to say (if we are allowed to speak at all), what we can do and where we can go, etc. But here's the thing: control is rooted in fear. What we are afraid of, we desperately try to manage and control because then we can direct or suppress its power over us. And from what I've studied and seen, it is clear to me that culture has always been afraid of women. Why is that? What could culture possibly have to fear from women? Let's start by taking a look at some powerful, influential women in history:

CLEOPATRA

As an Egyptian queen and the last Pharaoh of ancient Egypt, she sought to defend Egypt from the growing Roman Empire. She married her brother (yes, true story) and he had her exiled, so she aligned herself with Caesar who in turn had giant forces that overtook her brother, so she was restored to her kingdom. This brought peace to the nation for a time. Caesar was eventually assassinated. Tensions grew in the country and Cleopatra began a relationship with Mark Antony, a Roman general. A civil war ensued in Egypt due to this relationship and Augustus Caesar, his rival, who believed he would give Rome over to the Egyptian empire. So much mystique has been written about her, for example, in Plutarch's Lives: Life of Mark Antony, Plutarch wrote: "For (as they say) it was not because her [Cleopatra's] beauty itself was so striking that it stunned the onlooker, but the inescapable impression produced by daily contact with her: the attractiveness in the persuasiveness of her talk, and the character that surrounded her conversation was stimulating. It was a pleasure to hear the sound of her voice, and she tuned her tongue like a many stringed instrument expertly to whatever language she chose...." She was the sole reason for an entire civil war in her country. Her image was put on Egyptian coins, yet she committed suicide after she was taken in battle. She affected and directly influenced the course of two kingdoms. She was an influencer.

QUEEN MARY I OF ENGLAND

Queen Mary was the firstborn child of King Henry VIII. She was the first woman to succeed at claiming the throne of England. She spent years fighting for her rights as royalty and is remembered for her restoration of Roman Catholicism. Due to her strict religious beliefs and her persecution of protestants, she gained the name, "Bloody Mary," beheaded many, and had over 280 religious dissenters burned at the stake. As a woman, she influenced such support for her beliefs that she mustered an army to fight the reigning king in order to become the first ruling queen and protect Roman Catholic beliefs. She was an influencer.

MARILYN MONROE

A pop culture icon and a sex symbol in the 1950s, Marilyn became famous for playing the "dumb blonde." Her beauty, success and fame influenced an entire generation of women, teaching that "playing dumb" is a part of sex appeal. Despite being rumored to be linked with the most influential people of the time, Marilyn died unexpectedly, struggling with reported substance abuse, depression, and anxiety. Women to this day dress like this icon, believing that dressing as a pin-up girl and looking the part will make you the most desired among women. For better or worse, she was an influencer.

ROSA PARKS

An African American civil rights' activist, Rosa Parks is famous for her refusal to relinquish her seat on the bus to a white man. Three of the four African Americans asked to move did get up, but Rosa Parks remained. She described her motivation for staying seated in her autobiography, Rosa Parks: My Story. "People always say that I didn't give up my seat because I was tired, but that isn't true. I was not tired physically, or no more tired than I usually was at the end of a working day. I was not old, although some people have an image of me being old then, I was forty-two. No, the only tired I was, was tired of giving in." Her refusal launched one of the most successful mass movements against racial segregation in our history. Her actions have left a lasting legacy for civil rights movements around the world. She was an influencer.

ESTHER

Queen Esther was commissioned by Mordecai to be courageous and go before the king to save the Jews. Mordecai could not influence the king, but Queen Esther could.

> *"For if you keep silent at this time, relief and deliverance shall arise for the Jews from elsewhere, but you and your father's house will perish. And who knows but that you have come to the kingdom for such a time as this and for this very occasion?" Esther 4:14 [AMPC]*

Because Esther laid her life on the line for others, she affected the king, and saved the entire Jewish race. She was an influencer.

DEBORAH

In a time where women had no power or authority to rule, Deborah, under the anointing of God, summoned Barak to gather 10,000 men to go to war against Sisera, the Canaanite general. She believed God, stepped out with her influence, and convinced Barak to fight against the Canaanites who had held them under oppression for twenty years.

> *"And she sent and called Barak son of Abinoam*
> *from Kedesh in Naphtali and said to him, Has*
> *not the Lord, the God of Israel, commanded*
> *[you], Go, gather your men at Mount Tabor,*
> *taking 10,000 men from the tribes of Naphtali*
> *and Zebulun?" Judges 4:6 [AMPC]*

God went before Barak, and chapter 5 tells us even the stars in heaven fought the Canaanites, and their bodies washed away in the river. She listened and obeyed God. He used her to influence Barak, and through her, God's people were freed from the evil King Jabin. She was an influencer.

DELILAH

Delilah is not remembered fondly, but we can see in the Word how her influence changed a giant of a man. The Philistines wanted to overpower Samson. They thought like the serpent that they would go through the woman. They offered Delilah money and the rest is history. Day after day she begged Samson to tell her the secret of his great strength:

> *"And when she pressed him day after day with*

*her words and urged him, he was vexed to
death. Then he told her all his mind and said to
her, A razor has never come upon my head, for
I have been a Nazarite to God from my birth. If
I am shaved, then my strength will go from me,
and I shall become weak and be like any other
man." Judges 16:16-17 [AMPC]*

Delilah used that information against him. She cut his hair, then Samson was captured, and his eyes were bored out. His great strength left him. She was an influencer.

~

Women have deeply influenced the course of history. These are but a few examples of the powerful influence women have and how these women have affected their families, cultures and even kingdoms. The enemy is right to be afraid of us. That's why I believe so much effort has been put forth in controlling, directing and suppressing women.

*But we must remember: "For we do not wrestle
against flesh and blood, but against princi-
palities, against powers, against rulers of the
darkness of this age, against spiritual hosts of
wickedness in the heavenly places." Ephesians
6:12 [NKJV]*

The enemy has been lying to us from the beginning. He tells us we don't matter, we cannot make a difference, but the early church tells us a different story. During Jesus' time, there was a woman at the well who changed the world.

The woman at the well had led a sinful life, but after meeting Jesus, she genuinely repented and converted to the Christian faith. Once she was baptized she was given the name "Photini" and she turned the place where she lived upside down for Jesus. After she met Christ she converted her five sisters and two sons and they all became tireless evangelists for Jesus. At the time, Emperor Nero was brutal with those of the Christian faith, yet Photini persisted in her influence and miracles.

One story of her miracles includes Nero ordering her fingers beat with rods for over an hour, yet not one finger was broken. He ordered beatings for two more hours and she walked away without broken bones. She could not be stopped. Her passion to proclaim Christ brought her before kings and nations. It's time to reposition our perspective of women to that of Photini in the early church portrayed in the book of Acts.

It's time we knew and embraced the power of our influence as well. It is time we stood up in the power and purpose of who we are and walked boldly in who God created us to be.

We are influencers. We have been given the power to influence others, and we have been given the choice to determine if the power will be used for good or evil. It's a gift to have this much power and it's a giant responsibility each day as to how we will influence those in our circle.

How will you influence? Will you be courageous like Esther and be open to change if God is asking you to do something that scares you? Will you be bold and confident always seeking God and answering the call like Deborah? Will you be led by feelings and society's desires like Delilah? Will the power of getting your own way rule the way you influence like Cleopatra? Will religion determine your choices like Queen Mary? Will injustice awaken you to rise up like Rosa Parks? Or will comparing and competing with Hollywood's idea of beauty influence your choices?

It's a power too big to choose on our own. Thankfully, we have all the help we need. It was never meant to be navigated without the Holy Spirit's grace and counsel. Choose this day to let God lead you no matter how you feel. Know a great gift of power has been given to you. You can make a difference in yourself, your family, your friends and community, and even in the course of kingdoms today. Exercise that power with responsibility and excellence.

Chapter 2

This World Needs Us
It's Time to Care

One needs look no further than our phones today to see the state of our world. Crimes of sin and hate, depression and suicide, greed and corruption, starvation, oppression, genocides, religious wars, school shootings. Pointless, needless destruction is all around us. You hear of it on social media. You see the effects of it and commentary about it on television shows and films. News channels, articles, and videos show us how fallen we are and how much we need Jesus as our savior.

We need women of influence to step up and be His hands and feet.

The Power of Belonging
by Philipa A. Booyens

I'm a screenplay writer and for one of the projects I completed, I had to dive deep into the character and backstories of Eric Harris and Dylan Klebold, the shooters responsible for the Columbine shooting in Littleton, Colorado on April 20th, 1999. I found some very startling consistencies between them and other mass murders that I studied for the project. One of those consistencies was that they all seemed to have experienced significant rejection from women, to the point where these mass murderers even cited this rejection as a reason for their hate for the world and the crimes they committed.

I do not believe there could ever be justification for crimes such as mass murder, but I want to again address the influence and power of women. Rejection can influence powerfully. And here's the thing: God does not reject us. He told the thief on the cross that "today you will be with me in paradise." He clothed the prostitute and stood against her accusers. He ate with tax collectors and sinners. He was called a "friend of sinners" and he created a massive following that truly changed the world and the course of history.

Do you know how Jesus did that? He loved people.

We are created in the image of God. Therefore, we are world changers too. We can change the world for the better.

I've personally seen how love and acceptance from women has changed lives. Growing up, there was a boy in my middle school class who, at the time, was kind of scary. He was vulgar, angry, big and talked about the weapons he had in his home often. Looking back now -- after my writing research -- I can see how this boy could have turned out. But what happened is a very different story because, the next year, a few girls and I decided to be his friends. We created a group and brought him in. He had acceptance and belonging; people that genuinely loved him as a friend and a human being. And he changed. The love and belonging he had gave him security in who he was and purpose in what he was called to do. His fierce personality became protective; he literally fought for us. His intelligence and passion for weapons were steered to a more purposeful degree and job. I truly am so proud and thankful for who he is and to have had such a great friend.

We could have rejected him or even just ignored him, and I don't know how he would have ended up. I'm thankful we will never know, because even when he wasn't that lovable, we loved him. This was one of the times I think we got it right because we did what Jesus does for us. I know how powerful and transformative love and acceptance can be. It's part of our power of influence and it has never been more needed or important.

I'm Sorry Isn't Enough

by Katie Walker

How many more news reports of child abuse, innocent killings, or any injustice will we wake up to before we do something? In 2013, I starred in a film bringing awareness to child sex trafficking. This was the first time I had been exposed to this horrific crime on a deep level. After much research, and many meetings with victims, pimps, and counselors... I was undone. I was emotionally distraught and utterly hopeless in the immensity of this issue ever being resolved. The very last scene I filmed in the movie was of Amber (my on-screen daughter played by Nicole Smolen) being brought back to my husband and I, where we see her for the first time since her abduction and abuse. My lines in the script were beautifully written but all I remember being able to say in the moment was, "I'm so sorry," over and over.

I drove home away from set and cried most of the way home. I cried every day. I'd replay scenes in my head and find myself in carpool picking up my own kids weeping. Something had to be done. "I'm sorry" just wasn't making a difference. I knew I had to do something to help. I began with what was in my hands. The film, 8 Days, that we made was a tool right in front of me to use to bring awareness to parents and teens. I could make a difference. And by God's grace, I have.

I've been on a campaign ever since, using the power of influence God has given me to speak to teens, parents, organizations, talk shows and government officials about this crime. I haven't looked back. Brothels have been shut down. Women have been rescued and freed from sexual abuse and slavery. Women and men have come forward with their own stories of abuse, freeing them from the bondage of silence and shame. Men and women have started their own organizations and projects to fight this crime. People have been set free from pornography addiction and contributing to the demand and abuse of these victims. The film and issue has gotten national and international attention from talk shows, reviews, and governmental agencies all because a small group of committed citizens used their power of influence to help these victims.

All the time and sacrifice away from my family to promote the film and travel to different engagements was fueled by the passionate hope that only God can give. He gives us all the help we need and provides what we need to do all that we are called to do because He is concerned about the one, the heart that is lost and broken. He goes after the one and He has given us the power of influence to do the same.

There has never been a time when women were more needed. What injustices do you see? What tools are in front of you?

God brought the issue of sex trafficking to us over and over again and we had no idea what to do about it. So, as we prayed and sought God for answers, He answered us each very clearly. This is important to Me. These victims are important. I've given you the tools to do this. Their stories need to be told. If you don't do it, who will?

Do you not like what you see in the world? Do not ignore or condemn it. You have the power to change it. It's time we are fully awake and aware of His purposes and plans for each of us.

Chapter 3

Your Identity

Do You Know Who You Are?

There is power in our identity. Every time I hear the question, "Do you know who you are?" I think of the Disney movie Moana and the climax scene and song, "Know Who You Are." In the scene, after Moana has crossed the horizon to find and save Te Fiti (the story's goddess of creation), she encounters instead the villain Te Ka (the story's goddess of fire and lava). Moana realizes that after Te Fiti's heart was stolen, she transformed from the goddess of creation - who created the islands - to destroying the islands as the goddess of lava. Moana confronts the lava goddess and gives her the heart that was stolen from her with the words, "I know your name. They have stolen the heart from inside you. But this does not define you. This is not who you are. You know who you are." And with those words and the heart restored, the goddess of fire and lava once again becomes the goddess of creation.

Though I do not believe in Polynesian mythology or Disney's version of it, I recognize the power of the story and the power of our identity and knowing who we are. This story illustrates this so clearly. Just like Te Fiti/Te Ka, knowing our identity can change us from destroying the world to restoring it. No matter how we have been hurt, what we have been told, what has happened to us, how we feel or even how we act, there is a unique and powerful design inside of each of us that is needed in this world.

We need to know who we are.

WE ARE CREATED IN THE IMAGE OF GOD

In the beginning of Genesis, God says,

> *"Let Us make man in Our image, according to Our likeness; let them have dominion over the fish of the sea, over the birds of the air, and over the cattle, over all the earth and over every creeping thing that creeps on the earth." Genesis 1:26 [NKJV]*

We can never truly know who we are until we know who He is.

To the God who calls himself, "I AM WHO I AM," you can bet identity is very important to who He is, and it is crucial for us to know who we are and why we are here. Here are but a few important characteristics of the God we are created like:

- God Is Truth - *Psalm 117:2; Jeremiah 10:10*
- God is Light - *1 John 1:5*
- God is Love - *1 John 4:8, 16*
- God Is Infinite - *Jeremiah 23:24; Psalm 147:5*
- God is All-Knowing - *1 John 3:20*
- God is All-Powerful - *Jeremiah 32:17, 27*
- God is Unequaled - *Isaiah 40:13-25*
- God Is Perfect - *1 Kings 8:27; Psalm 139*
- God Is a Most Pure Spirit - *John 4:24*
- God Does Not Change - *Numbers 23:19; Malachi 3:6; James 1:17*
- God Is Without Limit - *1 Kings 8:27; Jeremiah 23:23-24*
- God Is Eternal - *Psalm 90:2; 1 Timothy 1:17*

- God Is Incomprehensible - *Romans 11:33; Psalm 145:3*
- God Is the Almighty One - *Revelation 1:8; Revelation 4:8*
- God Is Most Wise - *Romans 16:27; Jude 1:25*
- God Is Most Holy - *Isaiah 6:3; Revelation 4:8*
- God Is Most Free - *Psalm 115:3*
- God Is Most Absolute - *Isaiah 44:6; Acts 17:24-25*
- God Is Most Loving - *1 John 4:8-10*
- God Is Merciful - *Exodus 34:6; Psalm 67:1; James 5:11*
- God Is Long-suffering - *Psalm 86:15; 2 Peters 3:15*
- God Abounds in Goodness - *Psalm 31:19; Psalm 52:1; Romans 11:22*
- God Is Forgiving - *Daniel 9:9; Ephesians 1:7; Psalm 86:5*
- God Is Just in All His Judgments - *Nehemiah 9:32-33; 2 Thessalonians 1:6*
- God Hates Sin - *Psalm 5:5-6; Habakkuk 1:13*
- God Is the Creator - *Isaiah 40:12, 22, 26*

We were created in His image. Sin has marred us, but it is God's purpose to restore us. To learn more about God and your identity, read and study the Bible. Another one of God's promises is that He rewards those who seek Him (Hebrews 11:6).

WE HAVE BEEN GIVEN POWER & AUTHORITY TO TAKE DOMINION

That is what He told us from the very beginning. Power and authority are granted. Dominion is taken. Because we have been given power and authority we must make the choice to take dominion over the changes we want to see in this world. We have been given the green light by God to move and take kingdoms for Him.

*"Sonship [and daughtership] is so important
that all creation is presently crying out for the
manifestation of the mature sons of God." Romans 8:19 [TPT]*

Our souls cry out to be free from the bondage of corruption, and it is time the children of God take dominion!

WE ARE CREATORS

Knowing that we are created in the image of God (Genesis 1:26) and that God spoke and the world was created (Genesis 1), I believe very strongly that what we believe and speak creates our environments. The book of Proverbs even tells us that:

*"Death and life are in the power of the tongue."
Proverbs 18:21 [NKJV]*

I used to skip over that verse, thinking it was a beautiful metaphor or an exaggeration to make a point. But after studying scientific research on spoken words, music and beliefs and their effects on water, health and the human body, I now one hundred percent believe that death and life are literally in the power of the tongue.

It makes sense that since we were made in the image of God, when we speak, we influence and create our environments. That's part of our design. It's part of who we are. We have been given the power to influence our environments mightily. Jesus said,

*"For assuredly, I say to you, whoever says to
this mountain, 'Be removed and be cast into the*

sea,' and does not doubt in his heart, but believes
that those things he says will be done, he will
have whatever he says." Mark 11:23 [NKJV]

Woman of Influence, what are you believing and speaking? What environment are you creating? You were designed with the power to move mountains. It's time to move them.

WE ARE HIS BRIDE

The Hebrew word meaning "it is finished" has another definition - "my bride." When Jesus said, "it is finished" on the cross, could the last words of Jesus also be crying out for His bride? His thoughts were of you while He was on the cross.

If God tells us, *"Don't be yoked together with unbelievers. For what do righteousness and wickedness have in common? Or what fellowship can light have with darkness?" 2 Corinthians 6:14 [NIV]*, don't you think He would only provide a bride for His son with those who believe? He prepares us and helps us become the bright and shining bride to be able to be "yoked" to God's perfect son.

WE ARE LOVED

Another crucial part of our identity is that we are loved. Recently, I was sitting in my room watching a YouTube video by Dr. Brian Simmons, the lead translator of The Passion Translation, on his teaching of the Song of Songs. I remember thinking from the deepest part of my heart, "Oh, I wish, I mean I really wish, God felt that way about me. I wish I was the Shulamite woman the King is talking to in the story!" As I finished saying those words, it's like time stood still for a moment and the very next words from Dr. Brian were, "and you are the Shulamite. You are the one God deeply desires and delights in. Male and female alike, God is ravished by you!"

I paused the video and cried. I remember saying out loud, "Are you sure? Can I really believe this about myself? It seems too good to be true and I don't really think my heart can take that kind of rejection. If I believe this, and if this 'Shulamite' doesn't represent how you feel about me, I need to know now!" And I cried. I cried because all of a sudden, deep in my spirit something was awakened. This revelation with all its intensity unlocked the deep places of my heart, this truth that was there all along. God was just waiting for me to receive it and he is waiting for you to receive it!

This is part of our identity and who we are.

WE ARE WARRIORS

> *"Of David. Praise be to the LORD my Rock, who*
> *trains my hands for war, my fingers for battle."*
> *Psalm 144:1 [NIV]*

Hands can be an emblem for relationship, or reaching out. And fingers can be a symbol for direction, connection, or giftings. He trains us for deep intimate relationship with Him to battle through the darkness in this world, and we overcome by His direction, through connecting with Him, and using the giftings He has graciously given us. Oh, my friend, you are equipped for war.

> *"Be strong, and let us fight bravely for our peo-*
> *ple and the cities of our God. The Lord will do*

what is good in His sight." 2 Samuel 10:12 [NIV]

We are called to fight for others. To restore hope and be a conduit for God to use. We must crush the fears we see in others, and use what God has given us to carry His glory. Our hearts must cry to wage war against the wickedness and evil we see and partner with Him to shake nations!

> *"Now you are ready, bride of the mountains, to come with me as we climb the highest peaks together. Come with me through the archway of trust. We will look down from the crest of the glistening mounts and from the summit of our sublime sanctuary. Together we will wage war in the lion's den and the leopard's lair as they watch nightly for their prey." Song of Songs 4:8 [TPT]*

You are a warrior.

WE ARE DAUGHTERS OF THE KING

> *"The King's daughter is all glorious within..." Psalm 45:13a [NASB, 1977]*

> *"Now if we are children, then we are heirs - heirs of God and co-heirs with Christ..." Romans 8:17a [NIV]*

You have been grafted into the bloodline of Christ. Don't live another day with an orphan mentality. Recite these truths over and over until you cannot help but act as the royalty you are. Being a daughter of the King is not based on you, your actions, or your behavior. It is based on who He is. This gracious King of kings calls you His, and you must come to a place in your heart where you call Him yours. It is a divine union, not meant to understand, but intended to live within.

"... Fear not ... I have called you by your name;
you are Mine." Isaiah 43:1b [AMPC]

You are His DNA now; a daughter of the Most High King.

WE ARE NEVER ALONE

The enemy of our heart plans and strategizes to make you believe you are alone in life. He constantly reminds you that your circumstances will not change, that you are unworthy, not needed and have no purpose. God says differently:

"And be sure of this: I am with you always, even
to the end of the age." Matthew 28:20b [NLT]

He is with you in this life and with you once you pass on to eternity. He is with you in every trial, struggle, and circumstance that presents itself to you. He reaffirms you to not be afraid.

"When you go out to battle against your enemies
and see horses and chariots and people more
numerous than you, do not be afraid of them;
for the LORD your God, who brought you up
from the land of Egypt, is with you." Deuterono-
my 20:1 [NASB]

People call us by our mess and remember us that way for years, but God doesn't. People pick out our weaknesses, but God doesn't see them. His love locked on you before you could even fail. He enjoys you even when you feel like a failure. You are not a problem or a project; you are a partner. He whispers in your ear: you are lovely. He sees the inner beauty inside of each of us. He sees us as He has created us to be: made in his image, creators, His bride, beloved, daughters of the king, warriors, and always by His side. This is who we are, how we were designed and how God sees us.

One of the biggest lies we've been told is that we (as women) do not matter as much; that we are not important. We can be our own worst enemy by agreeing with what Satan says of us. By trusting the Liar and our feelings of low self-worth, we have ignored and abandoned our identity and who God created us to be. We cannot afford to do that anymore. I love the words from the movie Gladiator, "What we do echoes in eternity." They ring true for us today and always. What we choose to believe and do determines who we become, and in turn those affect everything and everyone around us. We must choose to surrender, believe and move in our identity and who God made us to be.

SURRENDER

> *"For my thoughts are not your thoughts, neither are your ways my ways," declares the Lord. As the heavens are higher than the earth, so are my ways higher than your ways and my thoughts than your thoughts." Isaiah 55:8-9 [NIV]*

You do not have to understand everything. In fact, you cannot understand everything. You must trust and believe Him and His word. With all my heart I want to encourage you to say, "Yes." Surrender what you think, how you will look, trust Him and step out. Surrendering your opinions to Him will help you see Him in all His faithfulness. The world will fade away, and you will see the power you walk in, and how to influence others with God's grace and favor.

Surrender is about relationship. I know Him, and because I know Him, I can trust Him. To build this relationship, spend time with Him, pray, talk, listen and read His word. We can trust Him because His word says,

> *"Give God the right to direct your life and as you*
> *trust Him along the way you'll find He pulled it*
> *off perfectly!" Psalm 37:5 [TPT].*

You can trust and surrender to Him. The world needs you. You will influence others today; influence them to fall in love with Jesus. This love walk has completely changed my world, my thought pattern, and transformed my life to a life alive, full of passion, and courage. I am a walking transformation, because I surrendered.

I have to surrender and choose it daily. Make the choice to believe in Him, to seek Him, to surrender every desire you have to Him and watch the amazing adventure you will have. He says,

> *"For I know the thoughts I think toward you,*
> *says the Lord, thoughts of peace and not evil, to*
> *give you a future and a hope." Jeremiah 29:11*
> *[NKJV]*

BELIEVE

You must believe who He is, what He says, what He thinks, and how He feels. It goes back to what Jesus said,

> *"For assuredly, I say to you, if you have faith as a mustard seed, you will say to this mountain, 'Move from here to there,' and it will move; and nothing will be impossible for you." Matthew 17:20 [NKJV]*

Nothing will be impossible for you, but you have to believe it. You have a choice. You can believe in who He is and what He says about you, move in that power and change this place; or you can reject all of it. You can be like Te Fiti (Moana's goddess of creation) or you can be like Te Ka (Moana's goddess of destruction). Know who you are, who you truly are. Believe it and believe in Him. In that lies your power to do the impossible.

MOVE

The miracle is in the movement.

> *"[Jesus] said to the man, "stretch out your hand." He stretched it out, and his hand was completely restored." Mark 3:5 [NIV]*

The man with the withered hand had not been physically able to do what God told him to do, yet he began to move and try to hold his hand out. Within the movement his miracle happened.

That is Jesus. He does the miracle when we move. Do not wait around for your miracle, step out and trust God to do it as you move.

Believe, surrender, and move into your future with great hope. You are a creator, a bride, unconditionally loved, a conquering warrior, exquisite royalty, and never alone. You have been given the power and authority to take dominion and change this place. The world needs you. It's in your power to make a difference. It's time to act.

Chapter 4

Your Purpose

Why are you here?

I have been asked more times than I can count by many teens, "How do I know God's purpose for me?" It is a question we all need an answer to,

> *"Where there is no vision, the people perish..."*
> *Proverbs 29:18 [KJV].*

People will seek it out by all means: through psychics, fortunes, prophets, prayer, life coaches, and mentors. Do you know why? Because we have purpose implanted deep within our hearts ready to be unlocked and the mystery to be solved, put there by the creator God. God says,

> *"Ask and it will be given to you; seek, and you*
> *will find; knock and it will be opened to you."*
> *Matthew 7:7 [NKJV].*

He has the answer. He IS the answer. And our purpose is to seek Him, because He promises you will find Him.

OUR LIFE PURPOSE

He wants to be around you and help you in every single desire of your heart. He desires your attention, responds gently to your broken heart, and fulfills every longing deep inside your heart. You have overcome Him. He says to you,

> *"Turn your eyes from me; I can't take it any-*
> *more! I can't resist the passion of these eyes I*
> *adore. Overpowered by a glance, My ravished*
> *heart undone. Held captive by your love, I am*
> *truly overcome!" Song of Songs 6:5 [TPT]*

You may think you are not worthy. He doesn't. Even though you have sinned and made mistakes, He still sees you as pure.

> *"Yes, you are my darling companion. You stand*
> *out from all the rest. For though the curse of sin*
> *surrounds you, Still you remain as pure as a lily,*
> *Even more than all the others." Song of Songs*
> *2:2 [TPT]*

He wants your companionship, so lean into Him and rely on Him to correct, empower, bless, and guide you. He says,

> *"I [the Lord] will instruct you and teach you in*
> *the way you should go; I will counsel you with*
> *my eye upon you." Psalm 32:8 [AMPC]*

DECIDE TO SEEK GOD FOR YOURSELF

My seeking-God journey began in 2011, when I decided I wanted to hear from God for myself. I grew up in church, and was fed the Word of God all of my life, but I relied on pastors and teachers for this knowledge.

I heard a preacher talking one time about God telling her to tell a woman that she will be pregnant and have a baby a year later. Unknowingly, the woman had struggled to become pregnant for years, and exactly as this pastor had spoken to her it happened.

The pastor shared her story of trusting in His voice and stepping out into obedience. I remember thinking, "I don't really hear God like that. Can I?" I'm not a preacher, just a regular woman, but I want to know God more. I wanted to know why was I here; I wanted to know many things. I still want to know so much more. I am always learning. I decided If I wanted to know this creator God more, I needed to read the bible and spend time with the Author. I became persistent at that day after day. At first, I did not notice hearing God, or anything really, but I did not stop, because I read and believed His promises,

"Draw near to God and He will draw near to you." James 4:8 [NKJV]

He was changing me. When my prayer was, "Lord, see if there is anything inside me that I am hiding from you. Help me let you in, change the evil thoughts in me, and lead me in your ways." He did. Slowly, different desires I had started disappearing. He was gentle, washing my heart from the inside out. I didn't know what to pray for, but He knew. I rested and read, and He did the rest. He keeps doing the rest while he refines and encourages me. He fills my anxious heart every single day when I scream out, "I can't hear you!" or "Did I hear you correctly?"

He gives me courage to write this book. A dream I never knew I had, as I had been told my entire life by teachers and my own English scores on tests that I could not write. One of the greatest benefits to seeking God and your purpose is how He can take all those words spoken over you, the judgments from others, the real cold hard facts from life and transform it. He shakes his head and says, "That's not what I have ever spoken over you." He is so incredibly faithful. Because of Him, I look at all the impossibilities of my life, and I look to Him with a smile, and I see deep in His heart, and say "I can't wait to see what you are going to do with this!" Give God your limitations and ask Him what He will do with them.

Don't know your purpose? Don't know why you are a certain way? Or why something happened to you? Ask God. Seek Him in His word. Pray and listen. He will answer.

YOUR PURPOSE DRIVEN LIFE IS WAITING FOR YOU

Living in your purpose and the power of your influence is abnormal, extraordinary, and exciting. Today, my friend Vernae called me. I was driving home from running errands. When I answered the phone, there wasn't a "hello," or "hey, what's going on!" She presented a very direct question. She said, "What word do you have for me?" Without a hesitation, God's promises started flowing through me so fast I was trying to remember them, so I could learn from them. We laughed and then she blessed me. She prayed so passionately for me I was in tears driving home. That is purpose. To be used by God, to be a blessing in someone's life, and to be blessed. It's a beautiful life. A purpose driven life, living with intentionality, living with and hosting the Holy God.

You are powerful, needed and equipped with all you need to live out your purpose. Begin by studying the word, praying the word, and acting on the Word.

STUDY THE WORD

Studying the word for me began by committing to reading the word. I made a decision to read the bible every day. I found that when reading, different verses would stand out. So, I would stop and look up different commentaries on those verses, or google that subject and listen to a sermon by a pastor to find more understanding. The underlying passion to study the word was to hear God for myself. After a while of this I began to know His nature, and could begin to discern more of His voice.

This will be a lifelong practice as the word is alive, and constantly maturing me.

> *"Truth's shining light guides me in my choices and decisions; the revelation of your Word makes my pathway clear." Psalm 119:105 [TPT]*

It is through studying the word that I developed a real relationship with God and learned the power of my influence. To learn about and move in your power, authority and so much more, seek Him by studying the Word.

PRAYING THE WORD

In my studies I always wanted to pray in line with God's will. I would stress myself out in prayer with thoughts: "Lord, this is what I want to happen; but not my will, your will." Then I would fret in my mind about what His will was on a particular subject. I finally realized that I would be in direct alignment with His will if I prayed the Word. So, I began memorizing scripture that stood out to me while I was reading, and I would begin praying that scripture. Then my faith would build because I knew the scripture was in line with His word, so what I prayed will happen.

> *"Now this is the confidence that we have in Him, that if we ask anything according to His will, He hears us. And if we know that He hears us,*

*whatever we ask, we know that we have the
petitions that we have asked of Him." 1 John
5:14-15 [NKJV]*

Start today by praying scripture over you, over your family and friends, and over our nation.

ACTING ON THE WORD

I sat down for an interview the other day for a magazine that covers 7 regions of the US talking about a short film I produced for a local film festival. The interviewer asked me why I had taken another role besides acting. For 7 years, he had only seen me on the camera side of films. I shared my story, "I said yes to producing a film because I felt a commission by God to invest my time in the people and story of this project." I certainly did not feel like I knew what to do, or that I had the skill set to do what was needed to be done, but I trusted I was hearing God's voice and I acted accordingly. Being confident to share your story with others is acting on God's word. For He tells us not to be timid. He will do it.

*"So he said to me, "This is what the LORD says
to Zerubbabel: Not by might, nor by power, but
by my Spirit, says the Lord of hosts." Zechariah
4:6 [NIV]*

This is not about you doing, it is about you being. Being in Him, and the doing will happen. You won't be able to not do.
I like to think of it as: what you are filled up with will come out. For my visual learners imagine you carrying a full cup of water and someone comes by you and bumps you, water will spill out. If you are full of the Word of

God and you get bumped, the Word of God spills out. You are a mirror image of Christ, He is within you. Let Him spill out onto others. Study, pray, and act on the Word of God!

Make a daily appointment with God and keep it. You will find your greatest adventure is in His presence. Build relationship with Him. It is the most crucial decision you will make in this life.

You are an influencer right where you are at this moment. Whether you are a stay at home mom, a professional working eighty hours a week or anything in between, you have a purpose and a powerful influence. This world needs you and it is up to you to be intentional and relentless in pursuing your purpose and moving in the power of your influence.

Chapter 5

Living in Your Purpose
Influencing the Influencers

S tudies have shown it takes at least twenty-one days to create a new habit. It is time for us to create some new ones. It is time to step into who we are called to be and influence the world around us for the better and the glory of God.

Here we have created a month-long study for you. Invest in yourself. Use these devotional days to spend time in the presence of God and allow Him to transform you. Be intentional. You are worth it. You are needed.

I did a video blog the other day for INsight Scene on "bringing your dance" that no matter what the day holds, we might have to take steps forward and backward, but we must bring our dance of joy and hope to each situation. You can see the video at www.insightscene.com. The world needs your dance, to influence those around you with God's transforming love. Say yes to His grace and walk with Him, choose Him daily and watch and see how He transforms your world! As you read the following devotionals, may you be blessed by INsight that encourages and exhorts your identity as an INfluencer!

We believe with all our heart that you will experience and understand the deepest love from the Father. We have no authority over what we don't love. Which means, if you don't know that you are loved, you can't effectively speak life, guidance, wisdom, and instruction into others' lives. So, when you want to reach out to the lost, celebrities, or anyone at all, really love them. That is Jesus' heart. No matter what they are doing or have done, love them. It gives you authority to speak into their lives and influence them.

My prayer as you read this devotional:

Oh Lord, open the eyes of our understanding to grasp the width, depth, height and breadth of Your love for us. May Your transforming grace and love surround and protect us all the days of our lives. May You rain down Your heavenly treasures upon us. May we seek You and delight in You every day. We believe You will achieve more than our greatest request, our most unbelievable dream, and exceed our wildest imagination. We believe You will outdo them all for us. May we be the influencers that You have destined for us to be. With You, nothing is impossible. In Jesus' Name, AMEN!

Day 1

You Are God's Favorite

by: Katie Walker

I was my kindergarten teacher's favorite. She asked me to be the leader in class, take the lunchroom spoon to the next class, letting them know it was their time to go to lunch. I remember her always smiling at me. I knew I was her favorite, so I couldn't wait until after class to help her clean the blackboard, or wipe off the desks. I anticipated her hugs, and the candy jar full of the greatest candy! No one could do anything to change my mind. If I didn't understand something, she would help me. I was completely secure, and gave my best, and was my best. I know I was in kindergarten, but because I knew I was favored, my walk is a little taller, my confidence is a little higher, and my courage was immeasurable.

There is a huge difference in knowing you are forgiven and knowing you are God's favorite. You may immediately think, "I believe I'm forgiven, but there is no way I am His favorite." You could be reliving things you've done in the past, what you are currently doing, or even thoughts you have that you believe disqualify you from being "a favorite."

I believe the Devil has completely imprisoned most Western Christians today with so much condemnation that it paralyzes us and keeps us from being able to live an extraordinary life, a life of being fully alive. The belief that God disapproves of us so strongly, that there is no way we can be His favorite, keeps us from ever jumping into our destiny.

You are His favorite, and there is nothing anyone can do about it, even you! He is God and He says,

*"For my thoughts are not your thoughts, Nor
are your ways My ways, says the Lord. For
as the Heavens are higher than the earth, So
are My ways higher than your ways, and my
thoughts than your thoughts." Isaiah 55:8-9
[NKJV]*

He is the God of all gods, Lord of Lords, Creator of all nations, He speaks, and it is so. He brings kings up and brings them down. He makes a way when there is no way. He carves a path when you only see mountains, He shines a light when all you see around you is darkness. He knows our anxious thoughts, broken hearts, biggest fears, yet He desires to bring peace, healing and courage to you. He wants you to walk a little taller, live in confidence, and be brave to reach your dreams. He is a tender shepherd and is compassionate in our weakness. He doesn't rebuke us in our busyness or distractions, but He continually calls us His "radiant one." I heard Dr. Brian Simmons once say, "He knows when we keep Him at arm's length and He still tells us we are radiant and beautiful to Him." He speaks directly to our rejection and shame. The son of God looks at you with all your failures, calling you "unrivaled in your beauty."

This is His thought toward you today, right where you are:

*"But one is my beloved dove-unrivaled in your
beauty, without compare, the perfect one, the
only one for me. Others see your beauty and
sing of your joy. Brides and queens chant your
praise: "How blessed is she!"" Song of Songs 6:9
[TPT]*

You are His FAVORITE! Be the woman of Influence today that knows she is loved. Walk in that confidence and pour out that same love to others. Remind your children they are God's favorite, tell a friend how valuable they are, use your words and gifts to bring encouragement to those around you today. So, when you hear His voice, don't be afraid to step forward. Arise and be brave. When you remember who He is, how He is the God of all nations, how He speaks and it is so, how He brings kings up and brings them down, how He is the God of angel armies, how He goes before you, you can be BRAVE. My friends, be courageous. He has a plan for you to achieve infinitely more than your greatest request, your most unbelievable dream, and your wildest imagination. He will out do them all.

Prayer: *Oh, God of my life, I'm so in need of you to fill me up with your love. Help me to know I am your favorite, so I can walk taller, live confidently, and have courage to do what I am called to do. I believe your Word, that you call me your radiant one, no matter how I feel, or what I think, I am beautiful, without compare. I cannot fail with you. I will walk today in your love knowing I am your favorite! In Jesus' Name, Amen!*

Day 2

You Are Powerful

by: Philipa A. Booyens

As I've been meditating on the power of influence that women have, I've been pondering and asking God, "Why have women been so oppressed throughout history?" And God revealed to me clearly that, "control is rooted in fear." He then showed me the image of a collared dog on a leash and said to my spirit, "Why do you put the dog on a leash?" I thought about it and came up with two reasons. The first is: we do not want the dog to get hurt. We do not want the dog to run away or run into the street and get hit by a car. The second is: we do not want the dog to hurt anyone. Many dogs have attacked people or even other animals. Both of these reasons come down to one thing: fear.

We know the dog has the power to hurt itself or others. We do not trust it. We are afraid for its wellbeing and the wellbeing of others; thus, we try to control it with a collar and a leash.

I am so glad we are not dogs; and, I am so glad God is not man. Even though we have often proven that as people we should not be trusted, God does not collar or cage us. He does not try and control or manipulate us.

Fear is not from God. God is love (1 John 4:8) and Perfect Love drives out all fear (1 John 4:18).

But to our enemy, the devil, fear is one of his most powerful weapons. I want you to truly realize that,

> *"we do not wrestle against flesh and blood, but*
> *against principalities, against powers, against*
> *the rulers of the darkness of this age, against*
> *spiritual hosts of wickedness in the heavenly*
> *places" Ephesians 6:12 [NKJV].*

The master manipulator has been using fear to control and direct culture. Throughout history, Satan has even used religion and twisted the word of God to oppress and control various people groups, including women, because he knows our value and how powerful we are.

The enemy is afraid of us. He is right to be afraid.

To me, having a history of blatant oppression is proof that we are powerful. That there is reason for our enemy to be afraid of us. So, when you encounter attack, know who your enemy is. It is not the person or people in front of you, but spiritual hosts of wickedness that are deathly afraid of you and the power you possess.

USE IT. God designed you to make a difference. You are powerful and you here for a reason. Right now. Today. In this moment and season, this community and country, to influence this place. To bring your dance, to shine light in the darkness, to heal the brokenhearted and set captives free. Move in that and know that when you do come against opposition, it is simply confirmation that you are moving in your destiny and calling. Remember, your enemy is a defeated foe. Read the end of the book. God won. Satan lost.

> *"What then shall we say to these things? If God*
> *is for us, who can be against us?" Romans 8:31*
> *[NKJV].*

Rise up and move, woman of INfluence. Light up the darkness and change this place!

Prayer: *Father God, we worship and thank you for who you are. That your plans and purposes are perfect. That your design for me is perfect and that you are always for us. I think you for the challenges and victories and I thank you that nothing can stand against you. Lord, I ask that my spirit come into alignment with Your will and way and that your purposes and plans be accomplished completely in me. Lord, I ask for the strength to rise and move boldly and powerfully in all You have called me to. And that those around me come to know you, love you and call you Lord.*

Day 3

You Rule Your Feelings

by: Katie Walker

Our entire body reacts based on how we feel. We make decisions all the time based on how we feel. It's a good or bad day based on how we feel. Are you getting the picture? Feelings can absolutely rule our world if we don't keep them in check.

I've said this before, I've been refined by this word, and I believe it wholeheartedly: "YOU CANNOT LIVE BY YOUR FEELINGS!"

Living by your feelings can take you to "crazy town" daily. You must discipline yourself to bypass your feelings and look inside to this question: What am I believing? Our feelings are based off of what we are believing to be truth.

This is something you must stay aware of and alert to on a daily basis. There are days I will wake up feeling down, or be fine all day, and all of a sudden feel depressed. I can go hours feeling this way; therefore, I influence all those in my circle negatively if I do not catch it. What I mean is, I must stop all that I'm doing and ask myself, "what are you believing that is making you feel this way?"

As Joyce Meyer teaches "You must think about what you are thinking about!" We must stay on guard.

> *For the weapons of our warfare are not carnal*
> *but mighty in God for pulling down strongholds,*
> *casting down arguments and every high thing*
> *that exalts itself against the knowledge of God,*

*bringing every thought into captivity to the obe-
dience of Christ, 2 Corinthians 10:4-5 [NKJV]*

The other day I was really tired. I had many things still left to finish
for the day and I had set aside some time to get it done that evening. The
doorbell rang, and a friend dropped by to pick her child up. I could tell
something was bothering her, but I dismissed it knowing I had to finish
the other tasks that I had planned.

But that's when I heard the sweet voice of the Holy Spirit ask, "Can I
interrupt you?" In all honesty, everything I had to do passed before my
eyes. I felt so tired. I wanted to scream, "NO!" because I really didn't feel
like doing another thing. But, I knew I could not let how I felt rule how I
acted. I have to trust God and obey. I looked at my friend, took and deep
breath, and asked her what was wrong. This precious friend had so many
heavy burdens on her, and she could barely say a word without a flood of
tears.

After we studied the word together and refreshed ourselves on what
promises we could hold onto in the Word for her situation, we were
both refreshed and full of energy for the rest of the evening. I still smile
thinking I had so much energy after she left I could go run a marathon.
I finished all I had to do that day with excellence. Do you see how you
must fight your feelings? Had I listened to how I felt, I would have missed
out on the blessing from God, and I'm betting I wouldn't have finished
my work for the day. The more you study the word of God, the more the
weapons of the word are inside you, and you will conquer every feeling.

The word of God transforms; let Him change you! You don't have
to compete for His attention. He loves when you seek Him for wisdom,
and He will surprise you with ideas. Take a moment and ask Him for the
desires of your heart. Jesus can radically change your life. He will take you
on a journey you couldn't dream. Choose Him and His ways today.

Say "yes" to the things you've never believed are even in your skill set, to things friends and family would say, "you can't do," knowing that Jesus can! He makes a way when there is no way. He carves a path when you only see mountains. He shines a light when only darkness surrounds. He is the adventure. What are you waiting for? Dive into the Word. The Word will take you on an adventure of a lifetime.

Prayer: *Jesus, you meet every and all my needs. You direct and teach me like a loving Father. I ask for your grace to help me always have a heart to be interrupted by you, and grace to not live and make decisions off my feelings. Let me not go to the left or the right willingly or unwillingly but be led every step of the way by you. I trust you. I say yes to you today! Your joy is my strength, and Your Word a lamp unto my feet. In Jesus' Name, Amen*

Day 4

You Have a Responsibility

by: Narmin Backus

How many times have you felt offended, hurt and misunderstood? How many times have you held grudges because of the offense? If we are honest, I think we would say too often. One of the last times I felt offended and ran to my Heavenly Father with a "legitimate" complaint, He lovingly showed to me something very unexpected and very brutally honest. The offense that infuriated me was the same one I often inflict on others.

The person who upset me was my dear aunt who was staying with us through the summer and whom I love very much. Some of the things that annoyed me over the course of her stay were very simple. Things like: loudness, constant need to talk and express oneself, interrupting, doing many things hurriedly, offering advice where it wasn't welcomed. I was getting mentally and spiritually tired from all of this "action."

One day I just ran to my Father complaining, "God I cannot take this anymore. Do You not see how tired I am? Why can she not see, act differently, and keep all her opinions to herself? I love her, but I am tired." And then suddenly I heard a still small voice asking me: "Are you any better? Don't you tire some people out? Do you do everything smoothly and in order? Narmin, how are you better?"

That reminded me of this verse:

"You, therefore, have no excuse, you who pass
judgment on someone else, for at whatever
point you judge another, you are condemning
yourself, because you who pass judgment do the
same things." Romans 2:1 [NIV]

This was a shock to me, but also a revelation. I asked forgiveness and continued to pray but this time, I prayed differently. I prayed for both of us for patience, for wisdom, to be able to see people with the Lord's eyes, and to be completely free of the Spirit of offense.

You see, my friend, the truth is, if you are sensitive in a particular area most likely you have a problem in that same area. What hurts you is what you have not let go of and if the focus is still on you, on your hurts and your grudges, then you are not free. If you take your focus off yourself and focus on your position in Christ, remembering who you are in Christ, you will be able to understand that all things are possible and that indeed you have freedom in Christ. He gives us more grace to fight any battle. If we stay stuck in our judgmental attitude, the same judgment will come towards us. We must remember that often we are blinded by our own sins, shortcomings, and misgivings. That is not the reason to judge others. Scripture teaches us humility.

"...God opposes the proud but shows favor to the
humble." James 4:6b [NIV]

If we do not humble ourselves before the Lord and follow men, it would be difficult to forgive and to operate in the Spirit of freedom and grace. And freedom is so very important, especially if we want to influence people. We have been given a great responsibility to be women of influence and we can not do this without the help of God.

"Now the Lord is the Spirit, and where the Spirit of the Lord is, there is freedom." 2 Corinthians 3:17 [NIV]

Prayer: *Lord, help us to dwell on the goodness and promises of the Lord, seeking our freedom and healing from the One,*

"who is able to do immeasurably more than all we ask or imagine, according to his power that is at work within us." Ephesians 3:20 [NIV].

Thank you, Lord. Amen.

Day 5

You Are His Darling

by: Katie Walker

I am so needy. I'll admit I feel like one of the most high-maintenance emotional humans that exist. It would be unfair to put the pressure on my husband or family to fill the needs I have that would complete the desires of my heart. Desires like constant affirmation, or attention, or praise. You get the picture. Complete high-maintenance! And when you are desperate to fill that need the world will entice you in every area through other people, career, or material things. But when I discovered my identity in Christ and began to allow Him to fill these needs, I was overwhelmed by His love. Completely captivated by Him. I wasn't seeking for my husband to say the "right" words, or demanding attention from my family, or trying to compete against others for that "perfect role." I was at peace, full of joy, and adventurously expectant to move into the calling that God had placed on my life.

When I began to focus my attention on God's word, and seek Him and His Presence every morning, I began to hear things inside my Spirit. For example, I woke one morning and in a soft voice before I stepped out of bed said, "Good morning, Lord!" and instantly I heard in my spirit, "I've been waiting for you to get up, so I could tell you how much I love you."

Honestly, I couldn't stop smiling. He does that to you, fills you up with so much joy, you walk around a little taller, with confidence that you are completely loved. God is the transformer. He is the strength, counsel, hope, and everything good on the inside. Are you lacking joy? Do you have peace? Ask Him to show you and tell you how He feels about you, but be ready. It is completely overwhelming, shocking, and all that your heart has ever wanted. It is everything and more that you could ever need. If your heart is broken and you feel it's beyond repair, trust Him to be so delicate with you. He will not leave you. He will not abandon you in your feelings. He will listen, and when you finish talking to Him, wait and listen to Him. He loves us even in all of our mess.

"All have sinned and fall short of the glory of God." Romans 3:22 [NIV]

To influence well, you must know how much you are loved, and you must know this passionate King that comes for you. Your limitations do not stop Him. Your shameful ways will not make Him quit pursuing you. You are the most beautiful, you are worth the blood of Jesus and He cherishes you in His heart.

"Look at you, my dearest darling, You are so lovely! You are beauty itself to me. Your passionate eyes are like loyal, gentle doves." Song of Songs 1:15 [TPT].

Can we pause right here and let those words wash over us? He is ravished by you, completely in love and desires for you to know it! Ask God to increase your faith. Step out when you don't know where you are going. Keep moving! You must live in the belief that God will carry you. God will give you the creative power to do what He has created you to do. You will be blessed. God will bring greatness in and through you. Be brave and be a blessing today.

Prayer: *Jesus, I draw near to you believing your word. Believing you love me no matter what I've done in the past or what I do in the future. My heart leaps with joy as your words give life to my heart. My soul awakens with a delight knowing you love me unconditionally. May I seek you more, and rest in your peace as I go about my day today. In Jesus' Name, Amen.*

Day 6

You Are Wonderfully Complex

by: Cheri Duckworth

I'm a mom. Like most moms, I wear many hats. When people ask me what I do, I often dread answering. Not because I'm ashamed or embarrassed, but because it's complicated. My week consists of time with the husband, parenting my kids, homeschooling, babysitting, hosting a television program, contributing to an online women's ministry (Shout out to INsight), working out, instructor and leadership team for Holy Yoga Ministries, duties as a director of a non-profit, and trying to be a good friend, daughter, etc. Needless to say, when the chance for a midweek dinner out with friends arises, I take it. It is a mini oasis. However, I have moments where my mind tries to steal my happy little getaway from me. Rude. Basically, my outing begins with me rushing out the door as soon as my husband walks in. I hop into my swagger wagon (that's a minivan) and turn up the radio. When I hit the road, it starts to happen. Somewhere between turning up the A/C and accelerating onto the entrance ramp, my mind begins to turn against me. One such moment occurred recently, when I was driving to meet one of my best friends. I began playing out the night in my head. I do this often. "What will I order? Hope there isn't a terrorist attack. Jesus, please don't let me have a wreck and die. I can't be late to dinner. What will we talk about when I get there? What if she's mad at me? What if we can't agree to disagree? What if I've disappointed her?"

All of a sudden, my oasis turned into a battlefield! I have just stressed my mind, body, and spirit with my own thoughts. Notice I end up focused on how my friend might feel about me by the end of the night, and it hasn't even started.

I hate disappointing people I love! It's a struggle for me. I've often fought my own mind judging me for not being able to be the "perfect" person I believe others need me to be. What a lie! Over the years I've worked hard on shedding the lie that I must be able to save my loved ones. I'm not Jesus! They have a savior and I'm NOT Him. I'm me. I can love them by trying to emulate Christ to the best of my human ability, but I am not the perfection of Jesus Christ. Nobody is. So, who is this "me" I speak of? I AM COMPLICATED. We all are! The Bible tells me so!

> "Thank you for making me wonderfully complex!" Psalm 139:14a [NLT]

I love Psalm 139! King David is a fascinating person of the Bible and he wrote some great Psalms. He was obviously a complicated individual. Born a shepherd boy, anointed as future king, hunted by King Saul, his best friend was the son of the man trying to kill him. He loved God, but committed murder and adultery. Did I mention he loved to dance naked and unashamed before the Lord?! Oh, and Jesus came from his lineage. COMPLICATED. Like me. I may not be a murder, but I'm sure my dancing before the Lord causes people to also question my sanity. When I read through the book of Psalms and hear David crying out to God in praise or in toil, I hear my own voice. My own complicated thoughts and emotions. How many times must David have played out in his head the conversations he would have with his BFF? Surely, he asked his share of "What ifs." BUT don't forget the word "wonderfully" that comes before the word complex in verse 14. It's a beautiful adverb! This means that my complexity is wonderful. God knows this about me because this is how he made me...us. We are all wonderfully complex. God, our Creator Father made us this way on purpose! In verse 13, David writes,

> *"You made all the delicate, inner parts of my*
> *body and knit me together in my mother's*
> *womb." Psalm 139:13 [NLT]*

David praises God for making him wonderfully complex! That means when we hear things like "Women are so complicated!" We can respond with "Isn't it wonderful!?" Instead of apologizing for who we are, we can embrace it like David did. The rest of verse 14 continues with,

> *"Your workmanship is marvelous—how well I*
> *know it." Psalm 139:14b [NLT]*

In other words, I know I'm complicated. It's wonderful! It's part of the marvelous work of God's own hands. This is me. This is who I am. Wonderfully complicated, a marvelous creation of God. It doesn't stop there....

> *"How precious are your thoughts about me,*
> *O God. They cannot be numbered! I can't even*
> *count them; they outnumber the grains of sand!*
> *And when I wake up, you are still with me!"*
> *Psalm 139:17-18 [NLT]*

God thinks I'm precious! He thinks about ME! A LOT. Then my favorite part is that He is with me. He is with you! Take courage my friends! The God of the Universe, of all creation, made you, knows you, thinks of you a lot, thinks you're marvelous and wonderful, and he is ALWAYS with you.

Prayer: *Dear Jesus, Precious Savior, my heart is full of gratitude to You for loving me as I am ... that You knew me before I was born and that You took time to put every complex detail of me together. Thank You for caring about who I am. Thank You for teaching me to embrace my identity as your marvelous, wonderful, and precious creation. There is none like You. I praise You for Your love. Let my mind have Your thoughts, my heart Your love, and my soul Your grace. In Your precious and holy Name I pray, Jesus, Amen.*

Day 7

You Are a Love Letter

by: Katie Walker

"...Your very lives are a love letter that anyone can read by just looking at you..." 2 Corinthians 3:1-3 [MSG]

I heard a beautiful message from Pastor DawnChéré Wilkerson of Vous Church in Miami, FL and she asked, "What does your letter look like?" She taught about context and content of your life's letter and I wanted to share a few of the truths that spoke so clearly to me.

As you know context is very important in understanding letters. What is the setting from which you live? After receiving Christ as Lord, the context of your letter changes. It is no longer shame, and destruction, it is now redemption. You are now forgiven of it all and you are a child of God.

God writes a letter in your life and it begins deep within your heart and spirit. He changes the context of your life from death to life. He rebuilds and rewires what you have torn down, and restores and heals the brokenness of your story. Every circumstance you face has to submit to the context of your life.

Content is also important in a letter. What content is in your letter?

What you focus on and what you consume is what you will create in your life. Stop comparing yourself to others and focus on what God is writing in your life. He writes the miraculous. He reminds you of the hope in Him. He showers His great love and mercy on you. Here is a little play on words. Be content with your content. Simply be yourself and let His Word transform your own thoughts and heart.

Woman of Influence, you are a precious love letter, written by the Spirit, filled with the Spirit, and signed and sealed by the Spirit. When you walk in this knowledge the world will see the name of the One who has written your letter and that your eyes are open to the destiny that He has planned for you. You are a letter that will change atmospheres, bring hope to your friends, and make a transforming difference in all those with whom you come into contact. May you be a walking advertisement for the name of Jesus today. Your loving Father smiles at the letter He has written over you, and cannot wait for all to read.

Do you think the disciples thought that 2000 years later we would be reading the letters they penned in the Word of God? I bet they couldn't even imagine what would become of their heart work. It's time to be overcome with imagining what God will do in your life and how He can turn around any challenge that is before you.

> *"He said to them, "Go into all the world and*
> *preach the gospel to all creation." Mark 16:15*
> *[NIV]*

Since you are a child of God, called to spread the words of Jesus far and wide, let God write the letter on your heart. Be the Woman of Influence you are destined to be and let your letter go forth into all the circles among which you live. We are desperate in this world to read the letters that God writes upon your heart. Be brave and courageous, my friend.

Prayer: *Oh Lord, You are my beloved and I am Yours. I believe and receive this truth and revelation that I am Your love letter to the world. You are maturing me on the way to where I am going. Lead, guide, and counsel me, because I trust in You. You are all I could ever want, draw me closer to You today, and may people see You in the letter that is my life. In Jesus' Name, Amen.*

Day 8

You Are Successful

by: Katy Lizardo de Contreras

About 10 years ago, I was experiencing a life full of stress, anxiety, frustration and failure. I was so confused as to why I was living that way, because I did not work for those results ... or so I thought.

Since I was a little girl, I've always been a purpose driven person, and a woman of passion, compassion, strength, and action. I was very used to thinking about what I wanted to reach and achieve, how to follow with a plan, stick to it and grasp everything or almost everything that I could focus on grasping. I was able to achieve so many things.

I reached many goals, especially in the educational and professional areas. At a very young age, I reached high executive positions at global companies, and the opportunity to be promoted every 18-24 months over and over again; it was like being on a racetrack winning medals all the time.

I was receiving many titles, certificates, recognition, trophies, medals and a lot of "glory". It felt good (for little moments), and then I would get back to wanting to achieve more and more.

The more I did and the more I accomplished, the more lonely, empty, sad, and depressed I felt. So, I decided to visit a therapist and even a psychiatrist to find out what was wrong with me and why I had those feelings.

To all my "friends," to the world, and all others, I had no reason to feel that because I was a very successful woman. I was "Super Woman" and I had it all. From a wonderful and handsome husband, a charming little boy, a beautiful home, a brand-new car, travels, shopping, an executive position, beauty....and "Jesus."

I tell you that the enemy had used me so much in making me believe that my priorities were on the right track, and that the path and life I had was the correct one.

Then it happened.

My marriage of 15 years was about to end in a divorce, my son started to gain weight and almost failed that school year, I was losing hair and gaining weight. Nothing and no one made me happy. I felt miserable and there was nothing that could comfort me.

My priorities back then had the following order:

1. Work and Career

2. Work and Career

3. Work and Career

4. My Son

5. Family and Relatives

6. My Husband

7. Myself

8. GOD

Yes, GOD was the last on my list, even though I used to say He was first and the center of my life.

One night while sleeping around 2 am, I heard something that woke me up. Seconds later, what comes to my mind was the book of Matthew chapter 6 verse 33. I quickly grabbed my Bible to read,

"But seek ye first the kingdom of God, and his righteousness; and all these things shall be added unto you." Matthew 6:33 [KJV]

In that same moment, I understood how my priorities were upside down and I received the revelation from the Lord about why I was feeling that way.

So, I encourage you, special, treasured, and loved women of GOD to seek the Lord and his kingdom FIRST, so you can experience a life of abundance producing the fruits of the Spirit. Be a blessing to others while you love and enjoy every second of your beautiful life no matter the circumstances.

Remember, if we put GOD as our highest priority and diligently seek Him, He will give us ALL the things we need, the desires He placed in our hearts, and so much more.

Prayer: *Heavenly Father of love and abundance, I come before your presence today to reach understanding and receive your revelation to be able to diligently put You first in my life. Guide me through your Holy Spirit to seek you with hunger, passion and joy. I understand that if I am honest enough to accept that my priorities are not in Your order, You will place it on my heart, so You truly become my center, my all, my first, in Jesus' Name, Amen.*

Day 9

You Are an Original

by: Katie Walker

Have you ever met someone that is trying hard to be someone they are not? It's a painful experience. Have you ever tried to be someone you are not? I am willing to bet we have all fallen into this trap. I know I have. I can actually remember quite a few times I've tried to impress people by hiding parts of myself because of insecurities or the thoughts that they would reject me if I were really myself.

I can remember a time I tried so hard to be so sophisticated, refined, and polished in my early twenties to impress people I did not know. I cringe even thinking about it now. I believed I wasn't enough, or original enough to be liked or favored. Can you relate?

This is what I would say to my young self:

"Own who you are. Own every single thing. Own where you are from, what has happened to you, and the choices you have made. You are an original. There is no one like you. Use the past to learn and grow. You can only make a difference being you, not being somebody else. In fact, you only have grace to be you."

In I Samuel 17, a young David speaks to the king with passion and basically says,

> "Let me fight this Philistine Goliath that defies
> the armies of the living God. When I kept my
> father's sheep and a bear or lion came and

took a lamb out of the flock I would catch it by the beard, kill it and deliver the lamb out of its mouth. The Lord who delivered me then will deliver me now."

Then King Saul, not quenching the spirit of this young David, said,

"...Go, and the Lord be with you!" 1 Samuel 17:37 [AMPC].

Then Saul had David dressed in a warrior's armor, but when David tried to move he could not. He wasn't used to them. David took them off gathered his stones with his pouch and his staff and took off after Goliath. David, being himself with all the grace given to him, killed Goliath and saved the nation of Israel from the Philistines.

David had the grace for victory in his life and actions when he was himself. He put on the armor the King recommended, but he couldn't move. He was able to take the giant down when he was himself. What armor are you putting on because society says this is the way we fight? What mask are you wearing to fit in with a certain group of people?

God has created you an original. You have the grace to be the best you. Take on today knowing you have grace being you and do just that. Be you today! The world needs an original.

Prayer: *Oh Lord, thank You for creating me an original. There is no one like me and you have given me all I need to be me. Help me remember this truth today and bring my best self to all those I encounter. You are my helper and counselor, help me and counsel me as I live for you today. In Jesus' Name, Amen.*

Day 16

You Are Needed

by: Halyn Rose

G rowing up, and even today, as I get dressed and put on my makeup, there is a picture I have in my head of my appearance: my messy bun is perfect and so is my makeup. As I look in the mirror, I realize that my looks are far from what I had imagined. Trying to meet my expectations of myself, I change into outfit after outfit while fixing my makeup in between. Tears start streaming down my face. I tell myself that I will never be everything that everyone wants me to be. I will always fall short. I have to tell myself that "I can get through this!" on a daily basis, having to counsel myself because I was too embarrassed to tell anyone else about my insecurities. But guess what? My insecurities are okay!

One of the most important tidbits of knowledge that you will ever come upon is the fact that you were made for a purpose! God needs you! Why else would he have created such a totally awesome person such as yourself?

As humans, we have a tendency to compare ourselves to others. As much as we struggle with it, that is just our human nature. But there IS hope! You do not have to feel trapped anymore. God tells us all through scripture that we are His and we are loved.

I believe that in each one of us is a mighty warrior! With our inner mighty warrior, we can conquer whatever feeling we have about ourselves that is incorrect, whether that thought be about our figures, a specific feature, or maybe your acceptance of yourself overall. God makes it very clear to us that He made us just how He wants us!

When God created all that we know today, did you ever stop to think that while all this was going on, he had YOU in mind? It is pretty amazing to think about. As He created the galaxies and the stars, He was thinking about you! Whether you prefer the ocean or forest, imagine the most beautiful place you have ever seen. Now think about how great Our God is to have created such a magnificent wonder. He is so great, that he placed you exactly where you are now for a definite purpose. You have a purpose and God has you exactly where He needs you. Let Him take control! Trust me... He knows what He's doing!

> *"For we are God's handiwork, created in Christ Jesus to do good works, which God prepared in advance for us to do." Ephesians 2:10 [NIV]*

Prayer: *Dear God, help me to lean more on you daily. Allow me to feel peace that you are in control. You have created each one of your children uniquely and with love. Help me to know that I am yours and yours alone. I pray that you comfort me and all those around me with the peace that you are our Lord and Savior. Thank you for my abundant blessings, family and friends. I love you, my Lord. In Jesus' Name, Amen!*

Day 11

You Are a Holy Vessel

by: Katie Walker

I f you ever want to know what's inside your heart all you have to do is notice what you are saying.

> *"...Out of the abundance of the heart the mouth speaks." Matthew 12:34 [NKJV]*

I'm always on my kids, "What are you watching on tv?" "What are you listening to?" "What are you saying to your friends?" I'm laughing as I type this, because I can see the eye roll and the look from them that says, "How many times are you going to ask those questions?" And without a beat, I remind them every single day and many times over that the world constantly bombards us with lies every single day. To combat that, we have got to put the word of God in us over and over. It is life-giving and fills the longings of our heart.

We are holy vessels and we must be very careful and guard everything we ingest by our ears, eyes, and mouth.

> *"Above all else, guard your heart, for everything you do flows from it." Proverbs 4:23 [NIV]*

The truth is, we will search our entire lives trying to fill the endless crevices of our heart with all the world has to offer until we turn aside and see what God has been trying to tell our heart since the day He formed us. We must turn aside like Moses did to see the burning bush. In Moses' day, bushes or trees would light on fire and burn up on a normal basis. I don't think it was a phenomenon to walk past a burning tree. In fact, at that time in his life, Moses was shepherding flocks and had probably passed this area many times over. Moses looked in passing to see that the bush was burning, but it was not consumed. He decided to turn aside and see why it didn't burn up.

But, notice this:

> *"When the Lord saw that he turned aside to look,*
> *God called out to him from the midst of the bush*
> *and said, "Moses, Moses!" and he said, "Here I*
> *am!"" Exodus 3:4 [NKJV]*

When you decide to turn aside from the world and all the distractions and call out to God, He will draw near to you! See and embrace how the King of kings views you. May you understand that you overwhelm Him. Understand that He writes a song and you are the theme of it.

> *"I am truly His rose, The very theme of His song.*
> *I am overshadowed by his love, Growing in the*
> *valley." Song of Songs 2:1 [TPT]*

You are His lily of the valley. You are made for Him. The perfect match with the perfect personality. God will take you on a journey with Him. We will learn, and He will hold us up. Get rid of inferiority, and insecurity where you watch others advance and you don't. God told Abraham "I will bless you," so receive by faith that God will bless you too. What are you waiting for? Jump in and let the King of Kings take you on an adventure.

Prayer: *Father, we need you. You are our every breath, and our every delight. Show us where we let the lies in our life and help guide us in your truth. Don't let us go the right or left willingly or unwillingly. Tattoo Your word across our hearts, and may we walk in wisdom. Drown out the negative and silence the noise, so we can hear what your Holy Spirit is saying to us. Search us and know us. See if there is any wickedness in us and lead us to the way everlasting. We choose to walk with you today and every day. In Jesus' Name, Amen.*

Day 12

You Have the Power of Choice

by: Beate Els

Life is all about choices. Every person builds his or her own life by using different tools and a certain type of foundation. We decide whether we use tools designed for destruction or for construction. Both of these tools are used for mass creation. The one creates to destroy, and the other creates to build. You are given the choice to decide whether you live a life of horrible destruction or wonderful creation.

We have the power to choose but no power to escape the necessity of choice.

When I was a bit younger, I had the responsibility to make decisions as the leader of the student body at my school. At the time, I was so scared of making the wrong choices that I sometimes tried to run from them. I still do that sometimes. Avoiding making a decision is also a choice.

My teacher said this thing in class one day that hit me like lightning and I'll never forget her words. She said: "Choices determine character." At that very moment, I was trying to sidestep some difficult decisions and I thought, "What does avoiding responsibilities say about me?" I went to speak to her personally about what she said, because I was stressed and didn't know what the right thing to do was. She directed me to this verse:

"In all your ways acknowledge Him, and He
shall direct your paths." Proverbs 3:6 [NKJV].

I never took that verse so seriously until that day and I can honestly say that decisions are a lot easier when God directs you.

Our choices are influenced by a lot of factors – friends, family, colleagues, employers, etc. These factors can motivate you to destruct or construct. They have influence in our decision making, but the most influential person you will ever encounter is YOU!

Choices are powerful; they give you the chance to affect change whether in your personal life or in the lives of those around you. God gave us this amazing power of choice to use to glorify His name. And with great power comes great responsibility. Our responsibility is thus accepting the consequences of the decisions we make and to use this power to the advantage of the kingdom of God.

Our life is a reflection of the choices we make. If you are unhappy with the results, make better choices. Pray for direction. With life comes choices. With choices comes change and with change comes fear, insecurity, sorrow and stress. So, what can we do? Hibernate? Take no risks for fear of failure? Some opt for that. They hold back. We are all guilty of this at times. A better idea however is to look up. Set your bearings on God, because unlike life (which is constantly changing), He remains the same.

Whenever I am feeling overwhelmed with decisions or the consequences of them, there is one Bible verse that really helps to relax me:

"Fear not for I am with you; do not be dismayed for I am your God. I will strengthen you, Yes, I will help you, I will uphold you with my righteous right hand." Isaiah 41:10 [NKJV]

God promises in His word that He will uphold us, that He will give us strength and "... the word of our God shall stand for ever" Isaiah 40:8 [KJV].

84

Prayer: *Dear God, thank you for the gift of choice. God help me today and every day to make better decisions. God help me to reflect Your glory in all I do and say. Thank you that I am not alone. I pray for your wisdom to guide me to make good decisions for myself, my family and those who surround me. God, make me aware of my thoughts and help me make choices that are in line with Your plan and purpose for my life. Amen.*

Day 13

You Have a Helper

by: Katie Walker

T he truth is we will search our entire lives trying to fill the endless crevices of our heart with all the world has to offer until we turn aside and let Him. Let Him fill you. Let Him love you. He is waiting to hear you say, "Yes, I will let you love me, and bring me to that place of intimacy with you!" After all, we are held up and together by Him.

> *"His left hand cradles my head while His right hand holds me close. I am at rest in this love." Song of Songs 2:6 [TPT].*

The left hand usually represents His mysteries (things we don't understand in life), and His right hand usually symbolizes Him catching us. He holds us in all the mysteries we can't understand, and we rest in His love. God lovingly reminds us how well He knows us. In the first four stanzas of Psalm 139, He states He knows who we are, He knows where we are, He knows what we are like, and He knows who He is making us to be. Rest in these promises and let Him love you!

> *"Lord, you know everything there is to know about me. You've examined my innermost being with your loving gaze. You perceive every movement of my heart and soul, and understand my*

every thought before it even enters my mind.
You are so intimately aware of me, Lord. You
read my heart like an open book and you know
all the words I'm about to speak before I even
start a sentence! You know every step I will take
before my journey even begins! You've gone into
my future to prepare the way, and in kindness
you follow behind me to spare me from the
harm of my past. With your hand of love upon
my life, you impart a blessing to me." Psalm
139:1-5 [TPT]

Open your heart and let Him draw you to Him. All He is waiting for is you to say is YES. Yes to Him, yes to the call on your life, yes to the unknown, yes to the wait. Before you know it, you'll be on an adventure filled with excitement, full of passion, and completely content in who you are. Your future is to dispense the glory wherever you are. Our destiny is to carry the fullness of Christ. Look at yourself in the mirror after saying yes to Him and say, "I'm becoming an entirely different person!" Christ's life within you is to be given to others, just as Jesus was given to us by the Father. We are to be a blessing to others as He was a blessing to us. We will become a refreshment and joy to the hearts of others. Let Him teach you who He is, what He thinks, and what He feels. The two things we need most are grace and truth. His presence releases both. Let Him draw you close. We are a nation of people desperate for truth. Let Him tell you everything He loves about you. Rest in Him and stop striving, He will be everything your heart craves. He will wipe away the fear you don't understand with His love, He will never lead you off the trail of your destiny, and He won't fail you in any season of your life. Let Him be your helper.

You are called, and you have a great destiny. Dream again, be hopeful, and turn to God. He fills that deepest longing, and greatest hurt. Let Him fill you and move with faith today. Believe that the God of Glory will come out of you. You will be a blessing to your family, to your friends, to your church, and to your community, because the God of Abraham's faith is in you. You are the answer. Go and be the blessing to others.

Prayer: *Oh Lord, you are the completion in our heart. You are all we need. You plus nothing is the answer. Give us grace today to let you in. Help us be open in every area of our life. Help us look to you in our pain and struggle and just "Let you." Help us say yes! In Jesus' Name, Amen!*

Day 14

You Can Change Your Perspective

by: Katie Walker

As a kid I had an overbite and I'm not exaggerating when I say it was bigger than a beaver. It was pretty cute as a baby, not so cute around age 10 and up. Nothing 2 full years of headgear around the clock and 4 years of braces couldn't correct! I'll never forget in early middle school this new cute boy moved to our school. He was tall, dark and handsome and everyone wanted to be his girlfriend. I remember praying and asking God for him to like me. I'll never forget the next day I smiled at him as big as I could, and he said, "Hey bugs!" Confused, I looked at him with a sweet smirk, and he said: "Yeah, you remind me of Bugs Bunny!" I laughed it off, and ran to the bathroom and looked at myself in the mirror.

Now let me stop right here and let you in on a secret blessing. For as long as I can remember, my mother would tell me every day how Jesus loved me and has a plan for me, and made me perfectly and wonderfully. When you hear something enough you begin to believe it. So, I know the following response was from the precious Lord and her life-giving words.

I looked into the mirror knowing and believing what my mom had told me about God, and I smiled as big as I could with all my big teeth and said with a squeal, "That boy gave me a nickname, no one else has one, and Bugs Bunny is my favorite cartoon!" I ran out of the bathroom skipping.

As I look back on this story, I tear up every time seeing that God taught me at an early age how to shift my mindset. I know the boy was making fun of me, I could have easily taken that as rejection, but I knew my identity. I knew who made me. I knew God had a plan for me not based on how I looked, and if I rested in His plan, I could enjoy life. I knew I had (and still have) a purpose and knowing that kept me from perishing. It is life-and-death knowledge!

Change your perspective. When ugly words come at you, you can stand in the beauty and truth of who you are. The truth is that God sets you up to succeed. He uniquely timed your birth so you could make the greatest impact. You are a child of the King, royalty, His chosen. He wants us doubly secure in His kindness towards us. He is unfailingly good, unchanging and constant. It's impossible for Him to see us any other way. No matter what people have said to you, or your behavior, nothing depends on what we do. Everything depends on who God is. He puts us in love. He puts us into Jesus. If Jesus goes by the name wonderful, we get to go by the name wonderful. It's an amazing, breathtaking, and awe-inspiring truth.

God gives us promises we can stand on when we face trials and need to shift our perspective. Whatever you may be facing or going through, ask God to help change your perspective, run with childlike faith toward Him in your need, and know that He responds with His word. His unchanging, perfect, and life-giving word. He is with you today and everyday making this promise:

> *"Listen to me, O house of Jacob, and all the*
> *remnant of the house of Israel, Who have been*
> *upheld by me from birth, who have been car-*
> *ried from the womb; Even to your gray hairs*
> *I will carry you! I have made, and I will bear;*
> *Even I will carry and deliver you." Isaiah 46:3-4*
> *[NKJV]*

This is your moment, a new beginning, a fresh start. God changes seasons and He guides history. Be encouraged. He is all for you! Grab your faith in Him, and take the adventure of your life! It is go time.

Prayer: *King of kings, we are prisoners of hope in your mighty life changing word. Thank you for your promises, your constant unconditional love, and power to shift our perspective. Change us, open our eyes to see the way you do about ourselves and others. May we walk out today with a different perspective a godly perspective full of joy and peace no matter what because we fully trust you will be with us leading and guiding us. In Jesus' Name, Amen.*

Day 15

You Were Made to Bloom

by: Nicole Smolen

During the past few months, I have experienced a wave of emotions: joy, sadness, peace, frustration, hope, and doubt. I started to question myself: "What are you doing with your life? Everyone else's dreams are coming true, except yours. You should just move on. Why waste any more time and energy on hopes?"

Often, it feels like the weight of the world is on my shoulders, but I am only 20 years old. Sure, I balance a lot: college, internships, acting, film-making, photography, and even an online accessory shop...but, I love what I do. Pure and simple. The trouble always begins with my own thoughts.

As I watched my best friends' careers and relationships skyrocket, I felt inadequate. Everything seemed to be happening for them. Although I was surrounded by people who love me, I felt incredibly alone. Shame crept into my life with thoughts like, "Stop feeling sorry for yourself. You should be happy." Even though I knew it was all wrong, I still felt pangs of sadness. I was stuck between high expectations and disappointments.

Then, I came across the phrase: "Bloom where you are planted." It gently reminded me that everything has a purpose. Instead of letting those negative thoughts and feelings bring me down, I let them bring me closer to God. I remembered that He is my rock—my salvation—and nothing can come between us.

Sometimes, we are so focused on the future that we miss out on living fully in the present moment. The only way to unlock blessings is to trust. Not in things, circumstances, people, or even yourself. Trust that God is in control. When you come to this realization, you can experience true freedom!

Stay patient and tend to what God has placed in your heart. Plant seeds of hope and faith. Watch them flourish in the light of His presence. Before God can change our circumstances, we must allow Him to change us.

If you are feeling lost today, start giving thanks. God will always make a way for you. You are His beloved child. You have a purpose. You are never alone.

> *"Trust in the Lord with all your heart and lean*
> *not on your own understanding; in all your*
> *ways submit to him, and he will make your*
> *paths straight." Proverbs 3:5-6 [NIV]*

In His perfect timing, your life will unfold with favor. Your dreams will no longer be dreams. They will become a beautiful new reality! Life is a grand adventure filled with possibility, and you are exactly where God intends you to be. So, cherish the journey, not the destination.

> *"Behold, I am doing a new thing; now it springs*
> *forth, do you not perceive it? I will make a way*
> *in the wilderness and rivers in the desert." Isaiah*
> *43:19 [ESV]*

Always remember to bloom where you are planted for He makes everything new.

Prayer: *Heavenly Father, thank You for choosing me. No matter what the storms of life may bring, I will plant seeds of hope. Give me the strength and courage to persevere in faith. Open the eyes of my heart, so I may see the good things You have in store for me. In Jesus' name. Amen!*

Day 16

You Are Free

by: Katie Walker

I'll never forget in early childhood, I came home from school one time with minus points on my paper in school because I had drawn animals and the world we live in using colors that were not real life. I had colored a giraffe purple, the dirt blue, and anything else you can think of as unrealistic as possible. I was devastated with this grade. I am a people pleaser by nature, and minus points just about ruined my life at the time. Not to mention, that one act instilled limits on my creativity. From then on, every picture, or story I would write was real life, or what I knew to be real life. Writing was a struggle, and drawing pictures ceased. I was uninterested in creating in school, but my playground became imaginary worlds and I would pretend for hours in my backyard.

In hindsight, this one act was a blessing in disguise, because the world of the imaginary must be cultivated to do what I do now. However, I want to draw attention to the freedom we need to be able to see and create in this world what is in our hearts. While I stopped creating on paper, I still created in my mind. In my mind, I could be free! You will never be free until you understand and believe that you are free. God tells us we are free. What does that actually mean?

> *"For the law of the Spirit of life in Christ Jesus has made me free from the law of sin and death." Romans 8:2 [NKJV]*

Believing in Jesus Christ and declaring Him to be your Lord and inviting Him in your life is freedom. It is a belonging - apart from this world, a security of truth, and an ever-present friend at all times. At that moment, you become alive. A new breath, fresh heart, and new life is your future.

The bondage of the world's rules no longer applies to you. Depression, shame, regret, and illness are just a few that must go. He gives you the power to overcome obstacles and bad behaviors of the past. God allows you, without hindrance, to grab hold of a brand-new life in Him. You become holy and work out and catch all the foxes that try to destroy the relationship between you and God.

> *"You must catch the troubling foxes, those sly little foxes that hinder our relationship. For they raid our budding vineyard of love to ruin what I've planted within you. Will you catch them and remove them for me? We will do it together."*
> *Song of Songs 2:15 [TPT]*

We all have different compromises in our life where we haven't allowed God to enter and change us. These "foxes" keep the fruit of the spirit from growing in us, and experience freedom in our lives. Once we are His, He frees us completely from our sin, and everything that entangles us. He gives us life with His mercy and grace ushering us into freedom and the destiny He had planned for us. This means your best is yet to come. You are not enslaved to anything or anyone. You are a courageous champion jumping into the calling He has on your life without fear. You may feel fear, but you must rely on His heart and not what you feel. He will show you How for you He is. You have a new relationship now, and you must understand,

"I know my lover is mine, and I have everything
in you, for we delight ourselves in each other."
Song of Songs 2:16 [TPT]

The one who delights in you wants you to live as one without hindrance or restraint. You are free to create your destiny. You may think you are unable to go for your dream, but my friend, we were all unable. But God will raise you up with His mighty strength and power and you will be the Woman of Influence you were created to be to awaken those around you. Your past doesn't matter. It ended with three nails. You only have a destiny. Walk in it today, and take those around you by the hand and escort them into theirs. You have the power. Go and Be.

Prayer: *Oh, Lord, may we know within our deepest heart how we are free. How You've conquered sin and death for us by the blood of Jesus, and You desire us to live life differently in this world. We are to live free from all that holds us captive, and steals our joy. Help us to see, and create heaven on earth in all Your glory. May we shine like You and live in the freedom to which You have called us. In Jesus' Name we pray, Amen.*

Day 17

You Can Re-evaluate

by: Kara Jenkins

Have you ever been so zoned out while driving down the road that you reach your destination and ask yourself, "How did I get here?" Maybe this is something that you are afraid to admit, but if you are like me and answered yes then you are not alone!

Often times we can get carried away with the distractions of our own life and the lives of others important to us. Our minds are the most powerful tool that God has given us. Our brains even communicate thousands of signals daily all throughout our bodies. If you've ever taken the time to read about human anatomy and the way we were all created by God, then you know how fascinating and complex it is. I'm not a doctor or a psychiatrist that can tell you why you've zoned out while driving, but I can tell you that it's okay. It's okay to question, "How did I get here?"

Have you ever asked that question while not driving? Maybe you've come to the realization that you are unsure how you got where you are in your marriage, or your career, or even your own health. Asking ourselves frequently, "How did I get here?" doesn't mean you've failed. In fact, it means you are actively taking a role in your mind and realizing that you want the answer to something bigger than your daily tasks. You want the answer to reevaluate your goals, your dreams, and your future; to reconnect with your loved ones and relationships; to reconnect with God and further grow your relationship with Christ. God is always there. Even when you may feel abandoned or alone, He has never left.

Here are two of my favorite verses to help you when you ask yourself, "How did I get here?"

This verse in Isaiah says,

> *"Whether you turn to the right or to the left,*
> *your ears will hear a voice behind you, saying,*
> *"This is the way; walk in it." Isaiah 30:21 [NIV]*

And then this Proverbs verse says,

> *"In their hearts humans plan their course, but*
> *the Lord establishes their steps." Proverbs 16:9*
> *[NIV]*

God guides our daily steps and he goes before us to make a path. So, I'll now ask you, "How did YOU get here?" How do you want to write the story of your life and tell others the answer to the simple, yet complex, question?

Prayer: *Lord, thank You for the peace, hope, and comfort that this message brings. I ask that You would continue to guide my steps daily, providing me with the wisdom to make sound decisions. Lord, thank You for always walking my path before me, and for ultimately walking with me through every trial and season of life. Thank You for your many blessings and for your comforting Spirit where I can come as a place of healing. Thank you for continuing to speak LIFE into me and allowing me to grow. Lord, I ask all these things in Your Name and speak words of affirmation over my daily decisions and steps. Amen.*

Day 18

You Have a Destiny

by: Katie Walker

I had an opportunity to produce a film this past year. I was walking into the meeting going over in my mind the many reasons why I couldn't say yes to this project. I have four children, I'm writing a book, hosting and managing INsight Scene, taking acting classes and auditioning, and I have never produced a film, I don't know what to do to be a good producer, and did I mention I had four children? I was about to open the door to walk in the meeting, and I was already feeling overwhelmed. In fact, I had already made my mind up to say "thanks, but no thanks."

That's when I felt a question bubble up in my heart from the Holy Spirit. "Will you ask me?" I stopped in my tracks and asked God with a heart poised to hear clearly His direction. So clearly were these words bursting in my spirit "invest in this person, don't go in there trying to impress them." Immediately the pressure was off. It wasn't about me. My insecurities of "knowing what to do" left, and I knew the Lord wanted me to be a part of this project. I boldly walked through the doors, and before he could even speak about the project I said yes. I laugh thinking how I must have sounded to this up and coming director. I was so full of confidence in God I blurted out, "God wants to confirm to you that you are doing what He has placed in your heart. You are supposed to write, act, and direct in movies. To prove it we will go next door and secure the first location."

He looked surprised but started packing his bags to go secure the first location. I sat there wondering what I said, and how I could take the words back and run. In my thoughts I said, "Lord, did you hear what I said, oh my goodness, HELP!" I surprised myself, but a crazy peace was over me.

We walked next door to an amazing building. They closed on Fridays at noon. It was Friday at 2:30pm. I would not let this deter my faith. I began to say, "Let's look through the window," when the door opened, and the owner was standing there. We explained we were making a film and would like to look at his space. Not only did he let us look, he opened his business to us for free for an entire week with filming crews in and out. I walked to my car that day praising God for moving, and manifesting His favor, and mostly for directing my heart to say yes.

Are you willing to say yes when your thoughts say, "Say no!" Are you willing to stop and ask for direction and bypass how you feel about it? Are you willing to trust God to teach you on the way? When you decide to jump, say "yes" even when your thoughts say "no," and trust God; watch what He does. He says,

> *"I will instruct you and teach you in the way you should go; I will counsel you with my loving eye on you." Psalm 32:8 [NIV]*

Be confident today knowing His loving eye is upon you. He wants to guide you into all of your greatest dreams. It's your turn to say yes. Be willing to do what you don't think you can do and watch the impossible happen as you let God direct your steps. It might feel uncomfortable, but He knows the future. He knows what projects you need to be involved in. He will set you up to succeed. You are valuable and needed. Be willing to stop and ask for His direction. Be willing to yield to your own thoughts and rest in His guidance. Your best is yet to come.

As you walk uprightly the Lord will not withhold one good thing from you. Believe that people will be blessed through your life. You will see things clearly, and see others through the lenses of tenderness and compassion. Rise up beloved and influence those around you to achieve their destiny.

Prayer: *Oh Lord, You are the greatest director we have. You lead, guide, and counsel us. Lead me today. Make us successful, open the doors to our dreams, and move the mountains, and give us grace to yield to you. May we turn our hearts to You and realize You guide us with Your loving eyes upon us. You don't miss a thing. Help me not to miss Your direction today. In Jesus' Name, Amen.*

Day 19

You Have a Standby

by: Narmin Backus

My dear friend, where do you look when you have a heartache, pain deep within you, storms raging around you, when life hurts and is hard to bear? In times of stress, crisis and pain we tend to look right or left, confused and frightened by what is happening around us. Worse yet, we look behind us, living in the past, asking ourselves, "what if?" or saying, "I should have..." Often we look ahead in total fear of tomorrow, trying to imagine what would happen if we do that or the other. We cannot get used the idea that we are not in control and every hour, every day and life itself belongs to the Lord, as He is our Master and Commander.

We also forget or are sometimes unaware of the fact that He is not a harsh taskmaster, but a loving, merciful, gracious Father who loves us more than we can see or understand. A few verses from the Gospel of Matthew come to mind when I think about this:

> *"Look at the birds of the air; they neither sow nor reap nor gather into barns, and yet your heavenly Father keeps feeding them. Are you not worth much more than they? And who of you by worrying and being anxious can add one unit of measure (cubit) to his stature or to the span of his life?" Matthew 6:26-27 [AMPC]*

These are the words of Jesus to His followers. They too were worried and concerned about tomorrow, just like you and I are sometimes, but the Lord graciously and patiently explained to them not to worry and gave a reason why. As I am sitting and typing these words I am reminded of the storms of my life, past and present, moreover outside of my window a real storm is raging and tearing our city apart. Hurricane Harvey hit Houston very hard and many people lost homes, cars, properties, and some lost their lives. Yet, I am reminded to look to Jesus, the author and finisher of our faith. Amidst devastating news, photos of our ravaged city submerged in water, I was reminded to look to Jesus, the Creator of the Universe, the One who commands the winds and the storms to be quiet, the One who truly has everything under His control, even when we do not see it in the natural.

I find comfort in these verses from the Gospel of Mark:

> *"A furious squall came up, and the waves broke over the boat, so that it was nearly swamped. Jesus was in the stern, sleeping on a cushion. The disciples woke him and said to him, "Teacher, don't you care if we drown?" He got up, rebuked the wind and said to the waves, "Quiet! Be still!" Then the wind died down and it was completely calm. He said to his disciples, "Why are you so afraid? Do you still have no faith?"" Mark 4:37-40 [NIV]*

How often do we look to Jesus and expect Him to answer us? How often do we cling to Him and fasten our gaze on Him alone? We are so used to carrying our own burdens, fixing our own problems, running to people first instead of running to the Lord, that we forget that He is always by our side, waiting to extend His hand of help. He wants to be all in all for us and indwell our being. The offer Jesus gave in the Gospel of Matthew is as real and available today, as it was when he spoke these words to His disciples:

> *"Come to me, all you who are weary and bur-*
> *dened, and I will give you rest. Take my yoke*
> *upon you and learn from me, for I am gentle*
> *and humble in heart, and you will find rest for*
> *your souls. For my yoke is easy and my burden*
> *is light." Matthew 11:28-30 [NIV]*

So now, I call upon you - all who are weary, afraid and have lost hope. Look at Jesus, look at the One who came to give you life abundantly, look to the One who knows your name and knows your sorrow, to the only One who can save you - look to the true Savior and trust Him with your all. Prayer: *Dear Lord, our Heavenly Father, thank you for being our Comforter, Provider, Restorer and Savior. We trust You and look to You for help and direction. Help us never lose heart, never look back in regret, but fast our eyes on our Savior Jesus Christ from whom all blessings flow. Uplift us with Your mighty hand. May You be glorified in all we do and say. In Jesus' name, Amen*

Day 20

You Are Wanted

by: Katie Walker

I was asked by a friend the other day, "Katie, would you rather be wanted or needed?" I responded, "Definitely wanted." My friend was in a job where he was so needed, but did not feel wanted. He didn't feel a part of the team, but his talent, and skill was needed to continue with the high level of product they were producing. It left him feeling used and rejected.

My initial response after hearing his story was to march myself into his job and demand they treat him better, remind them who is on their team, and give them a piece of my mind. Haha. But for real, that is how I felt However, I've learned that no matter how I feel I have to take these emotions to God to get clarity and truth before I make decisions that could create drama and embarrassing situations at the same time. Silently I was asking God how to handle this situation for my friend, when the Holy Spirit said, "Tell him that he is wanted. Tell him that he is wanted and needed. Tell him I've created him and given him these skills and talents to make a difference in culture, and no matter how he feels or how others treat him I want and need him." I reminded my friend of these words and hoped the truth resonated inside his heart.

Truth will set you free, and you must live today knowing you are wanted and needed for this time, this season. How can God reject what He loves? His love for you is so deep and wide we cannot even fathom or understand. We must ask and seek for God to reveal this truth to us.

"And may you have the power to understand,

as all God's people should, how wide, how long,
how high, and how deep his love is." Ephesians
3:18 [NLT]

At the end of Song of Solomon, the Shulamite bride finally realizes how God sees her and it completely sets her free from the rejection of others. She is now mature in the ways of God and walks in the knowledge that she is wanted and needed by the King of kings. She says,

"...This is how He sees me - I am the one who
brings Him bliss, Finding favor in His eyes."
Song of Songs 8:8-10 [TPT]

Oh, my friend, You are the one who brings Him bliss. You are wanted. You are needed. In spite of your weakness and flaws, He calls you beautiful. Know this truth deep in your heart, so you will be able to fight the rejection and lies that come against you in this life. The One who has called you is more powerful than any uncertainty you are facing. God's way is not mere talk, it's an empowered life. Today, walk in GOD-fidence as He is unchanging! He wants and desires you. It's time to make a difference at your workplace, in your family, and in your community for the better. Volunteer more, take time to listen to others, and remind those around you that they are needed and wanted. Your voice matters, so use it for good in your realm of influence.

Prayer: *Oh, Lord, come away with us today. Reset our negative thoughts with the truth of your word. You've given us a handbook of love to maneuver through this life and the lies and rejection that come against us. We believe we are wanted and needed by you. There is nothing this world has for me, but I have all things in you. May we take your love to the ends of the earth. In Jesus' Name, Amen.*

Day 21

You Have a Comforter

by: Ainsley Ross

When I was a kid, I remember going to the grocery store and the movie theater with my parents. It was so fun and exciting for many different reasons. One of the biggest reasons was the toy claw machine. The inside of that square box looked so inviting with all the colors, the plush animals, and prizes you could win.

One day I was playing, and I thought I had everything planned out. My Mom and Pops kept trying to help, but I wanted to be in control over the situation and do it myself. I was so focused on what I wanted that I did not listen to their advice or tips. So, I pressed the red drop button, and I just knew I was going to achieve my goal. SURPRISE! That did not happen... I was upset because I put a lot of thought into it. That's when my Pops stepped up and gave it a try.

It was out of my control. I feel like we do that a lot in life. We get so focused and determined to achieve a goal, and control the situation, that we block out and ignore the red flags. I feel like we often try to plan out and control our life, because we are too scared to act on faith.

Like relationships for example: don't try to plan out your relationship. What I mean by that is; it is okay to have goals and make smart choices, but don't plan out each and every step of your relationship. Don't box yourself in by saying you will only date (x, y, and z). God wants you to have more than you ever desire, imagine or fathom. By trying to control and make those plans, you are really just limiting yourself. You deserve SO MUCH more than your expectations, and God knows that. So, trust

Him. You are brave, pretty, incredible, and stronger than you give yourself credit for!

God, knows your strength, worth, heart, mind, and spirit. Do not be anxious. Just know that there are many blessings ahead. A great Bible verse that is comforting to me when I grow anxious about life:

> *"Cast all of your anxiety on Him because He*
> *cares for you." 1 Peter 5:7 [NIV]*

What has control over your life? Is it work, tv, social media, a relationship? What gives you headaches or makes your shoulders tense up? Make a list right now of everything you are struggling with control over in your life. It can be anything! Once your list is complete, I want you to tear out that piece of paper.

Now say this prayer over your list:

Prayer: *Dear God, these things I've listed have been occupying my mind, heart, and spirit. I feel the need to control these situations. When really, I'm trying to comfort myself by the lack of control I have. That's why God, I ask that you take this and fill me with the comfort in knowing that it's out of my control, because it's in Yours. Amen.*

After you have said your prayer, take that list and cut it up, bury it, or throw it in the trash. It's okay for things to be out of your control. Let God comfort you in knowing that all things are in His control. He is,

> *"One God and Father of all, who is over all and*
> *through all and in all." Ephesians 4:6 [NIV]*

God's got you.

Day 22

You Are Not Forgotten
by: Katie Walker

After thirty years of what seemed like a normal happy marriage my parents divorced. This left scars of heartbreak, anger, pain, and sadness in my life. All that I knew and believed in was simply taken from me. I was already an adult at this time, but it seemed as though everything I knew and trusted was a lie. I was left for a decade believing and doubting in God's ways, His love, and His healing. I would cry out to God and ask Him to help restore my family, and all I could feel was nothingness and a rage of anger. I had a new family of my own at the time and decided to focus on that and not deal with these nagging thoughts that God is not answering my prayers the way I wanted it.

The pain I felt was so loud, I couldn't hear anything else in my spirit except this thought: "I will take revenge. I will not let this go for the sake of justice, and the protection of my own heart." If I didn't see God's justice, then I would do it myself. For a decade, unfortunately, I wreaked havoc upon family members and my own heart. Every time there was a family get together, I wouldn't go, or I'd show up with a burning rage inside. It hurts even today remembering the pain. I was so broken. It hurt so bad. For a decade it never got better. My heart never healed. The pain was the same. Time did not heal all wounds. God had forgotten me, or so I thought.

In 2012, another family event was happening, and the anger and pain was just fresh as it was in the beginning. I couldn't take feeling this way anymore. It literally took my breath away. So, I sat in my car and I screamed at God. I said, "Help me, I'll do anything not to feel this way again!" and I cried. I heard nothing and for two hours I cried and went through all the reasons I was hurt, and why I needed to hold on to a little of the anger. All of the sudden, deep in my spirit, I heard, "What if you holding on to this is the reason why I can't move." I was so broken I yelled out, "Take it. I don't want revenge, I trust you, I want to forgive fully, and I want to be released from this bitterness."

It was in that moment something happened. All of a sudden peace and joy rushed in, my heart was restored with a fullness I can't explain, my eyes saw differently, and I loved. I loved so hard the people that had broken my heart. I looked up to thank Him and I heard these words, "You are not forgotten."

You, my friend, are not forgotten. You are not rejected even if you feel He is not responding the way you see it. He is walking with you, and waiting for you to cry out to Him. In that deep part of your heart give Him that brokenness and let Him restore you to fullness of joy and hope. God is the One who never leaves the one behind.

> *"...for He [God] Himself has said, I will not in any way fail you nor give you up nor leave you without support. [I will] not, [I will} not, [I will] not in any degree leave you helpless nor forsake nor let [you] down (relax My hold on you)! [Assuredly not!] Hebrews 13:5b [AMPC]*

Whether you feel forgotten or not He tells us,

> *"...And be sure of this: I am with you always, even to the end of the age." Matthew 28:20 [NLT]*

118

Yield and surrender to His love and let Him fill you with His fullness. It is life changing and joy exploding. His mercy is limitless; His faithfulness is so infinite; His goodness is unmovable. His judgments are full of wisdom, and His care and kindness leave no one forgotten. He has set you up to succeed! Rewire and renew your thoughts so you can walk out God's great plan for your life. Woman of Influence, God uniquely timed your birth so that your life would have the greatest impact. You were not created to make a dent, you were created to make a difference. Make one today.

Prayer: *Oh Lord, may we surrender our needs and hurts to you fully and completely. May we accept your love and grace and walk in forgiveness today. I pray a special anointing of your healing over our hearts today, so we can walk in truth that you could never forget us, and you care about every single pain and brokenness we have. Help us, heal us, and hold us today. In Jesus' Name we pray, Amen.*

Day 23

You Are Not Alone

by: Katie Walker

My home is surrounded by woods, so when the sun goes down it is pitch black besides what light the moon offers. We have two dogs that must be walked nightly. On occasion, one or both of my two younger children will walk with me outside. In the really dark patches of the driveway, I will feel little hands searching for me to hold their hand. No one, even me, likes walking into the shadows, or where we can't see. We can only imagine what wildlife is creeping or watching, and history at this home has proven every once in a while, a snake will show up on our path. The fear of the unknown, and our creative imagination can bring paralyzing fear that delays our destiny.

Much like life, I would prefer to hold someone's hand and be guided by a strong guardian that knows and sees into the unknown. We have been promised, as children of God, there is a counselor, helper, advocate, intercessor, standby, and strengthener who will never leave us. In fact, He goes before us, behind us, and encircles us.

> *"You've gone into my future to prepare the way, and in kindness you follow behind me to spare me from the harm of my past. With your hand of love upon my life, you impart a Father's blessing to me." Psalm 139:5 [TPT]*

121

Not only are we not alone, He imparts a father's blessing. It's too good to understand. It is wonderful and will bring you strength in the unknown.

My mother was leaving our home the other night. The moon was full, and she stopped walking to praise God for the creative beauty, when laying at her feet was a giant copperhead snake. If you don't know anything about this snake, they are deadly poisonous, and blend in with our concrete rock filled driveway. Had she not stopped because she was led to praise the Lord, I believe she would have easily stepped on this snake that would have swiftly attacked her. She was not alone. Hearing her scream, we quickly went running and my husband jumped through her car window like Bo and Luke Duke were famously known for doing in the show "Dukes of Hazzard." He flattened the snake doing the Indy 500 around our driveway, but not before that snake jumped and tried to attack the wheel of the car. You see the Lord knew what was lurking in the darkness, He guided my mom to safety, blessed us all by protecting her, and gave me the best memory and story to retell over and over how we are a family of snake killers using whatever is in our hands at the moment. You see praise was in my mother's hands, and car keys were in my husband's hands, and I was along for the ride.

Do not place your destiny calling on a shelf and say, "one day," because of fear of the unknown. Jump in the adventure of the unknown with confidence that you have a strong and wise guide. He will never leave you. He is the guide we need.

"Seek His will in all you do, and he will show you which path to take." Proverbs 3:6 [NLT].

And this:

"The steps of the God-pursuing ones follow firmly in the footsteps of the Lord. And God delights in every step they take to follow him. If they stumble badly they will still survive, for the Lord lifts them up with his hands." Psalm 37:23 [TPT]

Take your steps today boldly and with courage knowing they are ordered from God, He delights in your move of faith, and He will always be there to lift you up. I speak courage to you dear friends, to move today into the unknown.

Prayer: *Today, O, Lord, may there be a grace to receive your great love. I ask for grace to receive this message that we are not alone, and you walk with us encircling and protecting us. We delight knowing that even if we feel alone, we can reject that thought because we are confident you guide us always. We will step today with courage and joy in the unknown, believing you are already there. In Jesus' Name, Amen.*

Day 24

You Are Enough
by: Katie Walker

I was sitting in front of the mirror applying make up the other morning, and I could see every fine line in my face. Those magnifying mirrors really know how to accentuate everything you don't want to see. I remember lifting my eyebrows up thinking Botox would really help this, and not eating sugar would really help these puffy eyes, and maybe a cream would help keep my lipstick from running down all the lip lines, and the thoughts kept progressing so much so that I looked at myself and frowned. I was feeling pretty down about this aging process, and just then my youngest daughter comes in the room and walks right up to me smiling, reached out and squeezed that extra saggy skin on the back of my arm and laughed. Cue the feel sorry for myself music. All I could hear in my mind was, "Your best years are behind you. Just try to enjoy where you are." Well, this thought didn't sit well with me. All these thoughts didn't feel good, and started my day off with a mindset focused all about me and where I didn't measure up, and it was only 8am. Can you relate?

I decided I couldn't live with these thoughts any longer, and I wanted to deal with them once and for all. I spent a long monologue telling God how I felt this morning, and wanted to know what He thought. His first response was,

> *"My thoughts are nothing like your thoughts,*
> *says the Lord. And my ways are far beyond*
> *anything you could imagine." Isaiah 55:8 [NLT]*

I responded, "Then tell me what you think, because I'm really having a hard time with this." I waited to listen to what the Lord would say and all of a sudden, this revelation came pouring in. I think you will be surprised, and find freedom for yourself as you hear what the Lord taught me that day.

He taught me that the world tells you what is beautiful. The world advertises what is appealing to people. You have been conditioned to think once you age, you are no longer as beautiful. But, I created the aging process. It is divine, and I delight and enjoy where you are in each stage of your life. The world will only feed you lies, that you no longer are attractive, or enough. But when I look upon you, I see where you have been, where you are going, and who you are. I say, beauty is only found deep in the recesses of your heart, covered in Christ's blood, and is on display in front of my eyes. I see the beauty in you long before you even show signs of it on earth.

My friends, we are His beloved. We are enough, and He meets us right where we are. You see I could listen to what the world tells me about aging and what is beautiful, or I can listen to what God says. In Song of Songs the Shulamite bride talks of her immaturity, and her thoughts then, but she has come to realize how He sees her as His bride, and we must realize and declare this as well,

> *"This is how he sees me, I am the one who brings*
> *him bliss, finding favor in his eyes." Song of*
> *Songs 8:8-10 [TPT]*

We must now be the mature ones in the ways of God and proclaim that we are enough right where we are. We must realize that we are beyond beautiful to Him, and it is Him who matters - not the world. We should never fear other people's opinions of what is enough or even our own opinions and thoughts of who we are. He says,

"But I will show you whom you should fear:
Fear Him who, after your body has been killed,
has authority to throw you into hell. Yes, I tell
you, fear him." Luke 12:5 [NIV]

So, the next time I routinely put on my makeup and see the fine lines that have been created by years of life, I will smile and say in my mind that each line in my face is beautiful. That I am enough - as I am and where I am - to finish the destiny that God has before me today. I encourage you to do the same. Fight what the world tells you, combat the thoughts that do not lineup with the word of God, and share this truth with someone. Let's free women, including ourselves, from the lies that we believe to be true. You can make a difference right now by challenging the world's view, and reminding yourself and others of the real truth.

Remember: your best is yet to come, and you will influence those around you for good.

~

Prayer: *Oh, precious Savior and best friend, I thank You that You meet each of us where we are and You tell us that we are enough. You're the source we lean against, the one we trust, and the faithful king. You look upon us with Your loving eyes and love everything about us. Help us have Your thoughts today, and fight the lies of this world with Your truth. In Jesus' Name, Amen.*

Day 25

You Are a Woman of Faith

by: Karen Jenkins

Y ou are women of FAITH! Stand strong and be Full of FAITH! God doesn't respond to our needs, but He does respond to our faith. How big is your FAITH?

It was a Saturday night on July 17, 1993 that I gave birth to a beautiful healthy little boy. I took him home on a Sunday afternoon feeling blessed that our family of four was now complete. We had a beautiful little girl who was 3 and a half years old and a brand-new baby boy. Life was good!

On the following Monday morning, my mom called me into the nursery where she was changing my son's diaper to tell me he was bleeding and she felt like I should call the doctor. Feeling numb and tired I proceeded to contact the doctor's office. By the time the doctor called me back, Brandon had several more diapers full of blood. We took him to the doctor, only to be sent directly to the hospital. On the drive to the hospital, my baby became lifeless and short of breath.

As I entered the hospital emergency door, I discovered in a panic that the hospital was being remodeled and I was nowhere near the emergency room. I started screaming, "Help me! Somebody help me, my baby isn't breathing!" He had begun to turn blue in the face. God brought an angel that day to my rescue! A sweet lady took Brandon and begin to work on him immediately. Within minutes she had him upstairs in the NICU unit.

I found out later she was head nurse in the NICU. Miracle #1!

The doctors started testing him for everything possible that could be wrong. After 12 hours, he had stopped breathing sixty-four times. His heart had stopped, and his breathing had stopped. I think I learned that day how to have faith. I had relied on my dad who was a minister and a great man of faith, to always pray and have faith for me. But that day I realized, I had to rely on my faith as Brandon's mom, to pray a prayer of faith over him. I realized that day, my walk with God mattered more than ever.

My faith would either see us through, or I would lose my son. If I didn't lose him to death, I stood the chance of losing my normal, healthy baby to brain damage, heart damage, or some other loss of normal functionality. The doctor told us he would be slow to learn and develop at the very least. I stood that day and said, "NO! Not my baby!" I declared healing over his body. I declared he would fight for his life. I declared he would not just be normal, but he would succeed and be advanced in every way possible. The doctors said he would never play sports of any kind, and that he would struggle to function and be a normal kid. He would be on heart monitors for at least the first two years of his life. I stood that day and declared he would NOT be on heart monitors and he would be healed in Jesus' Name.

By September of that year, just a couple of months later, Brandon was off of all heart monitors, breathing on his own, functioning on his own. He played every sport as a youth. He graduated at age 15, and started college at age 15. I'd say that was above normal. He did not struggle, but excelled in all areas of his life. Faith took us through to victory and Faith will carry you through as well.

When our faith aligns with God, our needs are always met. I cry out to the Father, "I need, I need, I want, I want! God please do this or please do that!" I can just imagine God looking lovingly down from heaven saying, "Oh, honey, just have faith, just trust in me, seek me and you will find all the answers to your problems." For He has promised He will answer the prayers of His people. When my FAITH is bigger than my problem, I simply don't even have a problem any longer. If my Faith can be that God can and will do anything, for anything is possible with God, then my Faith has made me whole. I am complete in my FAITH.

> *"Then Jesus told them, "I tell you the truth, if you*
> *have faith and don't doubt, you can do things*
> *like this and much more. You can say to this*
> *mountain, "May you be lifted up and thrown*
> *into the sea," and it will happen." Matthew 21:21*
> *[NLT]*

God speaks, and things happen! When we speak out in Faith claiming our blessings and claiming the answer to our prayers, things change. There will be a shift in your thinking when you begin to think in FAITH terms. Don't allow anything to consume you or let you become overwhelmed. Trust in the Lord God Almighty and allow your heart, your mind, and your soul to have FAITH. We possess the power in our tongue to speak life or death. Speak LIFE! Have FAITH and truly believe that with God all things are possible! He is willing and able. Have crazy BIG FAITH in our Amazing GOD!

Prayer: *Father, I pray You show us all how to have more faith in You. Show us how to declare blessings over our families and over our situation. Faith is not measured in desire or needs, faith is measured by You, our heavenly Father. We can never have too much faith. Keep our eyes on You, and allow us to gain access to more Faith. Faith will lead us, Faith will sustain us, Faith will open doors, Faith will help us overcome our biggest fears and our worst nightmares. Faith is the key to any problem or need. We seek You, Father, for more faith. Give us faith, in Jesus' Name we pray. Amen!*

Day 26

You Are Valuable
by: Katie Walker

I magine you are standing in the center aisle of a grand ballroom. There is a royal throne at the end. On it sits the King of Kings and He is watching you. There are amazing, priceless gifts on either side of the aisle. These gifts are all your answered prayers, and more than you can imagine, hope, or dream. The king wants to give you each one. You can see these gifts and they are glorious, but nothing can deter your focus and eyes from the king. As you walk you notice your stride is graceful and spell binding. The king is enamored by you. He longs with great compassion to give you every gift. Every step you take, the excitement overwhelms Him. In that very moment, you realize you are His most valuable treasure and you know He would die for you. You long to know what you can do for Him, and without hesitation He answers your heart's question. He says, "Believe that you are my most valuable possession."

Can you imagine this scene, with you center stage? We need to be reminded of this daily. We are valuable, and we belong to the King of Kings. He tenderly cares for you. He loves the grace in your every step as you reach out to Him. You are beautiful and breathtaking to Him. His heart beats for you.

"My dearest one, Let me tell you how I see you,
You are so thrilling to me. To gaze upon you is
like looking at one of Pharaoh's finest horses. A

strong regal steed. Pulling his royal chariot."
Song of Songs 1:9 [TPT]

He sees us as a strong mare harnessed to His heart. He wants to draw you deep into his heart and take you into a new realm. Can you imagine what the King would reveal to you? In His presence angels bow, demonic princes tremble, our pride melts, and He would reveal everything He loves about you.

"Look at you my dearest darling, You are so lovely! You are beauty itself to me. Your passionate eyes are like loyal, gentle doves. Song of Songs 1:15 [TPT]

I always find this so mysterious, as these words are spoken to the immature one. This is how He speaks to us before He has even transformed us with His grace. These are the words He says, when He meets us right where we are, before you even show signs of living and loving Him.

He loves us in all our sin, finds us, draws us, then offers us real life. His heart burns for His bride. We are valuable and there is nothing we can do to change His mind. He may not like what we do, or how we behave at times, but He loves and leads us out of our own sinful flesh. Remind yourself how very valuable you are to Him and fight any thoughts that come against that truth.

Your true hero will come to your rescue. The Lord alone is your Savior. He sings a song over you, and His thoughts of you are so many we can't even count them.

"Many, O Lord my God, are Your wonderful works which you have done; And your thoughts

toward us cannot be recounted to you in or-
der; If I would declare and speak of them, They
are more than can be numbered." Psalm 40:5
[NKJV]

God concentrates on you. He is for you, doing what you can't do for yourself. We can trust Him.

"You've gone into my future to prepare the way,
and in kindness you follow behind me sparing
me from the harm of my past..." Psalm 139:5a
[TPT]

You have purpose. You have been called to a purpose, one that only you can do in your area of influence. God has called you and equipped you whether you feel it or not, whether you are living in that purpose or just now discovering it. You are needed. With God, impossibility vanishes! Be the breakthrough for someone. Remind your family, friends, coworkers how valuable they are. You could be the very influencer they need to bring about their own breakthrough. Rise up and speak out.

Prayer: *O Lord, You are wonderful, and your love is mysteriously capti-*
vating. If I were to search for all eternity long, I would find there is none
like you. I am overwhelmed that you call me valuable, and your heart
burns for me. I believe and ask for your grace to reveal more of this
wonderful love to my heart, so I can give to others what you give to me. I
believe I am valuable and belong to you, in Jesus' Name, Amen.

Day 27

You Have the Answer
by: Lori Carouthers

"Ask and it will be given to you; seek and you will
find; knock and the door will be opened to you."
Matthew 7:7 [NIV]

I want to encourage you to ask questions. Questions are powerful. Questions open doors. Questions give direction. Questions cause us to be thinkers. Questions are good, not disrespectful. Questions are part of our relationship with God. Asking God to help you with the stuff life brings is an act of faith. Over 20 years ago I had so many questions and I could not seem to get any answers to them. I would ask everyone that would listen - and still I was left with the same questions. So, finally, I had a "come to Jesus" meeting with Jesus. I let Him know that I needed some answers to my questions. I decided IF there were any answers to my questions I would find them in my Bible. I decided to read every page, every verse, every chapter in my Bible until I found all the answers to my questions.

Well, some of the questions just did not have answers, or they paled in His presence. But something happened in the course of my quest of answers that I did not expect or anticipate. I fell in love with the Word. You cannot separate the Word from who Jesus is. He IS the Word. He IS the Answer! Before I started this journey, I knew just enough of the Word to be dangerous. I knew enough scriptures to feel like I was a true Christian. I knew just enough Word to be complacent. I only had a few verses set to memory. I could only tell you a couple of "addresses" of the verses that I knew. I did not open my Bible every morning. I did not know how powerful the living and active word was in my everyday life. But the questions were the key to relationship with Jesus! I still had lots of questions after reading my Bible through, but I discovered that questions were the very thing that gave me the Answer.

This must be a lifestyle. I want to encourage you to get your Bible out every morning and "ask," "knock," and "seek" - you will receive from the Lord. There is no question too big or too small for the Lord. This is a promise given to all of us. If you ask, the door will be opened for you!

Prayer: *Jesus, You are the God of "More than enough". You said that if I would ask, that You would surpass anything I could even imagine! I thank You for Your presence in my life. I thank You that You care about all that concerns me. Help me to ask questions that bring me closer to You! Help me to knock on doors that are Your purpose for my life. I thank You, Jesus, that Your Word is living and active. I thank You that Your Word is light. Lead me today in Your ways...in Your Word. I love You, Jesus! Amen.*

Day 28

You Are An Ambassador
by: Katie Walker

I, along with my team at After Eden Productions, had the greatest opportunity to visit the United States Embassy in the Dominican Republic while traveling and promoting the 8 Days film. The US Government partnered together with the Dominican Republic to bring awareness to the crime of sex trafficking by having us tour and speak throughout the country on this uncomfortable topic. After experiencing this visit with the Ambassador at the Embassy, I couldn't help but compare the life we have as Christ's ambassadors.

> *"So we are Christ's ambassadors, God making His appeal as it were through us. We [as Christ's personal representatives] beg you for His sake to lay hold of the divine favor [now offered you] and be reconciled to God." 2 Corinthians 5:20 [AMPC]*

These are a few of the comparisons we are blessed to live as an Ambassador of Christ:

- The US ambassador had a direct line of contact with the President of the United States, and we have direct contact through our Savior Jesus Christ with God Almighty.

*"For through Him we both have access by one
Spirit to the Father." Ephesians 2:18 [NKJV]*

- The Ambassador had secret service protection everywhere they traveled and stayed while living in the foreign land. We can always come to the mercy seat of Christ and rest without fear, for He will hide, protect, and be our refuge in this world.

  *"His massive arms are wrapped around you,
  protecting you. You can run under his covering
  of majesty and hide. His arms of faithfulness are
  a shield keeping you from harm. You will never worry about an attack of demonic forces at
  night nor have to fear spirit of darkness coming
  against you." Psalm 91:4-5 [TPT]*

- The Ambassador of the United States helped aid Americans living and traveling outside the United States. We as Ambassadors of Christ have the perfect message with the perfect Messiah to help aid and bring hope to the broken and backsliding.

  *"For by grace you have been saved through
  faith, and not of yourselves; It is the gift of God,
  not of works, lest anyone should boast. For we
  are His workmanship, created in Christ Jesus
  for good works, which God prepared beforehand that we should walk in them." Ephesians
  2:8-10 [NKJV]*

- Lastly, while living in a foreign country, the United States Ambassadors are given a beautiful home and an interpreter to maneuver easily in the foreign country. We have been given the beautiful Holy Spirit to indwell us and interpret all of our needs.

> *"But the Helper, the Holy Spirit, whom the*
> *Father will send in My name, He will teach you*
> *all things, and bring to your remembrance all*
> *things that I said to you. John 14:26 [NKJV]*

Be bold today in the way you walk, talk, and conduct yourself reminding yourself you are an ambassador of the One who provides for us. It is God plus nothing equals all we need. He is our Counselor in good and bad situations, our Helper for all things, an Advocate always having our back, an Intercessor praying on our behalf, our Strengthener building muscles to finish this race well, and our Standby never leaving our side. Be courageous today!

Prayer: *Precious Holy Spirit, You are more wonderful than we can imagine. You direct us to Christ and pour truth in our hearts. Help us be the mirror image of Christ, that when people look to us today we could radiate the glory of the risen Savior. Thank you for all of the privileges and blessings of being an Ambassador of Christ. Help us to recognize this favor, walk in it daily, and represent You by Your grace. In Jesus' Name we pray, Amen.*

Day 29

You Have a Reason to Be Confident

by: Nise' Davies

Confidence is an important ingredient for success. As a former SAG agency owner, feature film Producer and Casting Director, I've seen first-hand how necessary that quality is for success. If you don't believe you are a great choice, why should anyone else? But how does a person "become" confident? I think there are two main areas we each must develop in order to become confident: **SKILLS** and **ATTITUDE**.

First, identify what skills are needed for the area where you want to succeed. For example, a person who wants to become an actor must develop their voice, their poise, and their acting skills. It takes an average of 10,000 hours of work or training to reach the master level of any skill. Most people will not put in the time required to develop their skills to the master level.

Second, examine your attitude. What do you believe about yourself? Many people have heard negative comments from friends, family and strangers that they have believed to be true. This is very damaging to your self-confidence if you choose to allow those comments and opinions to define you. For the truth about your self-worth, let's open the Bible to see what God says about you.

> *"For I know the plans I have for you," declares the Lord, "plans to prosper you and not to harm you, plans to give you hope and a future."*
> *Jeremiah 29:11 [NIV]*

"But God demonstrates his own love for us in this: While we were still sinners, Christ died for us." Romans 5:8 [NIV]

"But the very hairs of your head are all numbered. Do not fear therefore; you are of more value than many sparrows." Luke 12:7 [NKJV]

"You are wonderfully and fearfully made." Psalm 139:14 [NIV]

When you realize that you were created by the Creator of the Universe, that God calls you His daughter, that you are fearfully and wonderfully made, then you will realize that you have great value. In fact, you have eternal value. My goal as a talent developer and personal development coach was to help each person become so confident in who they are in Christ, and so confident in their skill set, that they could cheerfully applaud the greatness in others. Jealousy is only able to entrap you if you doubt your own value. When you know your value, you can joyfully appreciate the greatness in others without feeling that you are less important. You KNOW God has a special plan for you. You KNOW you were uniquely created by the God of the Universe and are valuable. There is no need to be jealous. Life is full of joy when jealousy is rejected.

Prayer: *Thank you Lord Jesus for loving me. Thank you for creating me and loving me. Thank you that you have a special plan for my life and that you are helping me every step of the way. Amen.*

Day 36

You Are Royalty
by: Katie Walker

I can remember as a child playing pretend constantly. We lived in a two-story home and I would pretend to be the queen of a great nation that was attacked by an evil King. I would be held as a prisoner until the handsome prince would come and save me. I'm sure I stole most of my stories from Disney somewhere between Rapunzel and Cinderella, but there was a constant theme. I was always a princess and I was always royalty. Little did I know as a child that this is our calling. It is who we are. It is what God calls us. He places a crown on our head and watches us grow up to fit into it.

> *"But you are a chosen generation, a royal priesthood, a holy nation, His own special people, that you may proclaim the praises of Him who called you out of darkness into His marvelous light;" 1 Peter 2:9 [NKJV]*

Royalty can be defined as people of royal blood or status. Because God has adopted us as His own we are grafted in as royalty. We are chosen, His own special people, and we have the honor to praise Him with our influence in this world. As we speak and live our life in God's Word, we are constantly growing in God's love and increasing more and more until it overflows. This overflow of love will bring rich revelation of spiritual insight in all things. We will come to know God fully as He imparts to us the deepest understanding of all he does.

We were once like my pretend play. We were attacked by the greatest deceiver of them all, Satan, and the handsome King/Prince (Jesus) had to save us all. He did it all. He did the work, and will complete the work in us. I pray just as Paul prays,

> *"I pray with great faith for you because I'm fully*
> *convinced that the One who began this glori-*
> *ous expression of grace in you will faithfully*
> *continue the process of maturing you through*
> *your union with him and will complete it at the*
> *unveiling of our Lord Jesus Christ!" Philippians*
> *1:6 [TPT]*

It is time to walk and live your life as royalty. You have a destiny and it will be to be like Christ. Are you living as royalty? Do you walk daily as the chosen daughter of the King? You have the influence of a holy nation. It is time to rise up and let Christ's power change our lives and the lives around us. It is important to be joyful as He transforms us from glory to glory to become like Him. We have a heavenly calling. It is time for us to love God and others more deeply and more passionately. You have a ministry. It time to call it forth and move towards this royal calling. Rise up, Royal Woman of Influence.

Prayer: *Heavenly Father, I pray that our love will increase and overflow. I pray for a rich revelation of insight. I pray to know You fully, to understand the deep mysteries of Your ways. I pray we choose the most excellent way, and we become pure without offense, and we are filled with Your righteousness. Thank You for completing the work You have begun in us. We will walk in this royal identity today. In Jesus' Name, Amen.*

Appendix A

Bible Versions Used

Scripture references throughout this devotional book are shown in italics and are followed by the specific reference as well as the Bible version in brackets, like this:

> *"I will instruct you and teach you in the way you should go; I will counsel you with my loving eye on you." Psalm 32:8 [NIV]*

The Bible versions referenced in this book are listed here with the abbreviations used.

AMPC Amplified Bible, Classic Edition KJV King James Version
NASB New American Standard Bible, 1995
NASB, 1977 New American Standard Bible, 1977
NIV New International Version
NKJV New King James Version
NLT New Living Translation
TPT The Passion Translation

About the Authors

Katie Walker

Katie Walker grew up in Shreveport, LA, and at an early age she began her love walk with Jesus Christ. She graduated from Louisiana State University and has since been an active participant and fundraiser with Major League Baseball during her husband's twelve year MLB career with the Boston Red Sox and Chicago Cubs. Katie has always had a love for acting. She is an avid actress and is drawn to projects that portray a purpose and message, especially ones that equip and encourage the millennial generation. She has completed and continues to study in acting methods and techniques. Katie was the supporting lead in the poignant film *8 Days* directed by Jaco Booyens. The film premiered throughout the United States and internationally in an effort to fight against the crime of sex trafficking. Katie has also appeared in several television commercials and is often featured in stage plays. She recently completed feature films *Because of Gracia* and *Color Me You* which both premiered in 2017. She has successfully produced her first film titled *My Father's Son* directed by Kyle Clements. In addition to acting and producing, Katie writes daily devotionals for social media outlets and is a host of INsight Scene, a social media entertainment platform encouraging women in their daily life. She is a sought after speaker for schools, churches and events to influence others to fulfill their destiny and see their purpose in God's plan for them. Katie currently lives in Shreveport, LA, with her husband, Todd Walker, and their four children.

Connect with Katie

twitter.com/insightwith_kt
facebook.com/katiewalker
instagram.com/insightwith_kt

About the Authors

Philipa A. Booyens

As the Creative Vice President of After Eden Pictures (www.afteredenpictures.com), Philipa grew up modeling, acting and working at her family agency in Franklin, Tennessee. An All-American in track and field, this cover girl was also a Jr. Olympic record holder, gold medalist and a collegiate scholarship athlete before becoming a published author and co-writing the Dove Award nominated feature film, "I'm Not Ashamed" (www.imnotashamedfilm.com). Philipa is also the writer for the feature film *8 Days* (www.8daysfilm.org), which was made to fight human trafficking and has been featured on numerous radio and television shows including Steve Harvey. Philipa's mission with After Eden Pictures is to transform culture through uplifting entertainment. She is a sought after speaker for schools, churches and events and is passionate about inspiring and commissioning people to be who God called them to be. Philipa resides in Dallas, Texas, with her husband Jaco and daughters, Arwyn and Elira.

Connect with Philipa

twitter.com/philipabooyens
facebook.com/philipa.booyens
instagram.com/philipabooyens

Women of Influence, rise up.
Connect with us at www.insightscene.com, where we network with and highlight inspiring women, ministries and projects from around the world to encourage and inspire you. Because empowered women, empower other women and together we can make a difference and change the world we live in.

twitter.com/INsightScene
facebook.com/INsightScene
instagram.com/INsightScene
INsightScene.tumblr.com
INsightSceneblog.wordpress.com